I Ate the Cake

A Journey for Justice

Darline Amos-McElroy

Published in the United States by DR Creative
Art

ISBN: 978-0-9820460-2-9

Dedication

To all the unheard and unloved, may God
grant peace through His justice.

Contents

I ATE THE CAKE

A Journey for Justice

Prologue

On a hot summer day in the Delta, my younger brother and sister, cousin, and I landed at the only park for Blacks in a subdivision known as Black Dog in Leland, Mississippi. The town, separated mostly into geographical sections according to our races, was populated by 3,000 people. We were in one of the Black folk's parts of the city where shotgun houses were standard. I did not visit the park often. Going outside was not my favorite, as I preferred to read or write. The opportunity to get the only chain-linked swing set available and the hotter than Hell aluminium slide and the iron merry-go-round, equally as hot, were a treat. Despite the intense heat, I enjoyed the moment.

Some children and their mother watched us from the outskirts of the park. After a phone call from the children's mother, my mother arrived at the park. Mama wanted us to apologize for throwing rocks at the lady's children, and everyone, except me, apologized. The rest of my siblings and cousin walked home while mom and I remained behind.

"Darline, please go ahead and apologize to her," my mom asked for the second time.

Staring directly into the "storyteller" eyes as we couldn't call anyone a liar, I firmly stated, "No, we weren't throwing rocks. It was her children who bothered us."

"Darline, as soon as you apologize, we can go." It was hot. Summer in Mississippi was humid, and a reminder to stay inside as the expectations of cool breezes were none. My mama's skin sweating yielded to the heat, but she remained calm, which sometimes she did not if you continued to disobey her. I knew I was pushing the limit but pushing the boundaries for what I believed was worth the standoff.

"No, we didn't do it," I repeated, knowing full well I was likely to get the whooping of my life. Children dared to respond in a negative way or perceived tone, and especially not to my mama. We certainly did not deny them in the presence of another adult. But it was a whooping I was willing to take, especially after those kids talked badly about my mom. And, to add insult to injury, their mother did too. Their mom teased us about my mom being spiritual and always praising God for everything, including her stockings. We were well known as church folks attending Sunday school and even occasional prayer breakfasts before Sunday school.

Being keenly aware of my mother's physical strength and disdain for disobedience, I still refused. Mom asked once more to apologize, and after another refusal, my mama apologized for me. A few moments later, she and I walked side by side, in silence, to the car. Although I was a slender child of average height, I walked next to my mom, feeling tall and full of confidence in my decision. At the same time, I expected the consequences of my refusal.

Once we were in the car, mama explained she knew I was telling the truth but just wanted to have peace with the lady. However, at ten years of age, what I wanted was simply the truth and fairness, and I was not apologizing for that. Truth brought my peace.

Chapter 1

The Art of Retaliation

The fiftieth birthday is a milestone for many. Some save and plan for at least a year to mark the momentous occasion. The golden birthday is a time of gratitude and reflection. As usual, the only plans I made were to celebrate with family and extended family from our church at one of my preferred seafood restaurants, Charlies, on lower Greenville Avenue in Dallas.

However, a few co-workers, Mandy, Sally, and Brock, carefully plan to make sure my birthday was one for the books. The Monday before my birthday, Mandy asked if I intended to be at work on Wednesday. Initially, I did not know why she asked as I had forgotten the big fifty was near. I told her yes, and she disclosed she was bringing the cake.

Mandy insisted we have a cake for my birthday the first time I stated that I did not want a cake. "Do you think this is about you?" With a slighted glance past my shoulders and gaining eye contact with Sally, Mandy continued, "It's not about you." She smiled, but her gaze and smile gained my attention.

I chuckled at Mandy's remark with awkwardness and requested, "Please don't buy me a cake. My family and I will celebrate my birthday with the Easter holiday this weekend." Though I sensed something wrong during the conversation with Mandy, I would have never expected a cake laced with alcohol. It was well known I did not indulge in alcohol, and Mandy knew my reasons. Before leaving the computer lab, Mandy glanced again at Sally.

Sally was Mandy's work shadow heeding to Mandy's every demand like a schoolgirl wanting to be with the popular girls. Sally, a teacher's aide, felt empowered by Mandy, often making demands through her. The previous year, Sally convinced Mandy to schedule the teachers to watch the children during cafeteria duty instead of the teacher's aides. Sally's constant agitation with the students often annoyed them and some of the adults; so, the children were better off. If I came to my office before the start of school, Sally, often annoyed with minority boys during morning computer-led tutorials, ranted and raved about the students whispering. It did not matter it was seven-thirty in the morning, and most students are excited to see their friends. She quickly escorted them to my office or the principals' offices, proclaiming the students' behavior deficiencies as she walked.

I felt as helpless as they did and allowed them to sit in my office, which they often desired to come. I took the opportunity of teaching them how to respond even when they were right. Watching minority children not understand the reality of their world was exhausting. Children at an early age do not have the skill set to respond to biases and stereotypes. They cannot always put a name to the mistreatment, so they express it in anger.

As an elementary school counselor, I was considered a part of the administrative team and office staff. Each team in the school decided how to celebrate team members' birthdays. At the beginning of each year, the secretary put slips of paper with our names in a plastic cup. The name pulled would be the person's responsibility to purchase a cake and set up the office area to celebrate the birthday. It was a tradition when I arrived. One in which the administrators and office staff were surprised I participated as the previous counselor had not.

Mandy drew my name to purchase a birthday cake. It was the second time she pulled my name, and the first time she bought the cake was without incident.

Mandy's behavior in the previous months caused suspicion of our work relationship. Mandy tailored her behaviors according to friendships. Her emotional inconsistencies confused me often; though some days were better than others, I wavered between like and dislike. I offered counsel at times to eventually learn it was only Mandy's games. With the new principal, Brock, her entitlement to power gradually unveiled. Parents called my office complaining about her interactions. Her curtness left people wondering how she managed to keep a leadership role. Mandy's frequent emotional antics stressed the environment, which was relieved when she attended off-campus training.

I was the only Black professional at the school when I first arrived. A Black custodian eventually transferred because of workplace conflict. The other minorities were those needed in the bilingual classes. I felt tremendous pressure being the only Black and hearing the frequent complaints of the previous counselor who was also Black. Coupled with this pressure were the past school experiences as a middle school teacher in the same district.

The office staff was White except for the bilingual office clerk the year I transferred as the school's counselor. Staff members warned to visit the office at least as possible. They were older White women who had seen a few principals come and go. As informed, they were challenging. Sometimes when I greeted them, they would not reply. Trying to gauge how to ask and when to ask questions was a job within itself. If I made a mistake, I did not have to guess how they felt.

It was my first school counseling position. Because I needed their assistance in many things, I submitted to persistent kindness. Eventually, they lightened up. They even began sharing recipes, discussing their families' engagements, grandchildren, and exchanging gifts. However, their boundaries remained very well established. Each day, I checked the room's pressure to determine how much to engage with them. The cost of gaining their workplace acceptance and a cordial environment was expensive. I took a little comfort in the fact their behaviors did not fluctuate between anyone.

My first year as a school counselor was enjoyable, although there was a learning curve. School counseling has many components, so I appreciated the staff's acceptance and kindness. I also gained an appreciation and understanding of leadership's role expectations.

I had a very supportive principal. He understood the importance of having a counselor and always refused to add responsibilities to diminish my role. The students' well-being centered his decision on protecting the counselor's time. He often encouraged me as a new counselor to learn the job, giving grace to myself. I was very grateful for his kindness, especially given the recent covertly abusive middle school principal's experiences. Mandy eventually persuaded him to require me to administer one of her testing assignments. She desired to shift all her testing responsibilities to me.

Mandy often complained about the principal. She regularly maintained how he reduced her leadership abilities to managing textbooks, testing, and discipline. Her limited involvement with instruction caused a barrier to interview well. According to Mandy, she did not know how to respond to classroom instructional best practices. Mandy, elated when he transferred to a prekindergarten center as a principal, taunted the move was a demotion.

The previous principal's replacement was Brock. Brock's request to meet during the summer for lunch before school resumed did not sit well. I considered the intrusion as my desire not to disrupt my summer any earlier than necessary. It was more about me than Brock. Not putting on decent clothes and makeup except Wednesdays and Sundays was a part of summer pleasures. However, I joined the lunch, not wanting to start on the wrong foot with the school's new principal.

My first encounter with Brock caused concern. He shared his personal life as though we had been long-time friends. He discussed how he and his wife did not often see each other because of her position in another school district. Busy schedules kept them apart. Since his drive was an hour, he stayed at a nearby hotel some nights to not make the commute. The long days at work and arriving early in the morning was not worth the drive home. As a part of what would become his almost monthly usual, he paid for all the lunch expenses and purchased the pizza I ordered for my children. I repeatedly requested he not buy the pizza as he joked about having to pay. I stressed my intentions to pay, but Brock took the tab.

Brock was not shy in promoting his trophies. He boasted of coming early to accomplish his work and be available later in the school day for the teachers and students. Frequent emails arriving as soon as six o'clock was his signature good morning. Brock made friends within the district quickly. He often conversed about people he knew, especially the school district's elementary human resource director. Because of appearing to have a strong desire for inclusion, I did not think much of his so-called friendships with people in the district.

Mandy complained of his continuous emails, texting before she was awake, and all the changes he made as a new principal. Many mornings she approached me with complaints about Brock the moment I arrived. Later in the year, Mandy connected with him and bragged about Brock's commitment to training her to become a principal. She often compared him to the previous principal. For unknown reasons, Mandy promoted Brock as one who cared about what was best for children. According to her, his goal was to eliminate people who did not have students' best interests. In an email to the staff once, she praised him as a strong leader.

It was the second semester of his first year my husband warned me to be careful. During the school counselor's appreciation week, Brock announced he would no longer be kind to me. I told him Brock joked often. Since Brock and I got along very well, I maintained the statement was a joke. He insisted no one joked in that way. From his experiences as a school leader, my husband cautioned me to remain alert. He also recalled my initial feelings of uneasiness with Brock and several staff members' concerns.

Work conversations usually occurred at home when an event was memorable. As educators, my husband and I discussed the complexities, nuances, and often comical events in school environments. If I had a reason to doubt Mandy's earlier conversation, he would tell me. I opened the discussion with Mandy's comment about the cake not being about me.

He laughed and gave a comparable experience after I mentioned maybe Mandy meant the office staff wanted cake. "Yeah, it's like when a friend plans a bachelor's party. It's not really about the bachelor, but more so about the guys attending."

I agreed with him, not wanting to seem overly critical at someone's generosity. I dismissed the uneasiness as being skeptical and allowing past experiences to influence my judgment. Mandy purchased a cake for my office birthday celebration the previous year, so I reasoned it was oversensitivity. Deciphering your intuition versus your skepticism becomes complicated after spending almost five years ducking and dodging bullets from a principal determined to force you to leave. As a counselor, I knew from my studies and experiences trauma entangles the past with the present.

The next morning did not bring any more of a relaxed mind than the day before. Seeing Mandy in the hallway, I engaged in conversation to share my husband's take on her comment. I wanted to gauge her reaction. She grinned without responding and walked off. Again, the unsettling feeling within came with a much stronger inclination.

She had given me reasons I was not internally able to defend until after the cake incident. Mandy often made unprofessional comments, such as comparing our salaries in others' presence when stressed about her responsibilities. Once, when a district's directive put a task as Mandy's responsibility, she slammed my office door because I refused to continue the assignment. She complained often about how I incorrectly completed the job, so I eagerly released her duty. When Mandy returned with her laptop, I watched an adult woman steam with anger and complain she did not know how to use the software to document the meeting.

Still, the idea she would give a cake laden with alcohol did not cross my mind as something Mandy would do. It is against board policy to have alcohol on the premises as well as distributing it.

On April 18, the morning of my birthday, as usual, I passed through the main office. The recently hired office aide sat at the greeting counter. After she said happy birthday, I stated that I hoped Mandy did not purchase a cake.

"She did. I saw it," she responded.

"Well, I'm not eating it. I told Mandy I didn't want a cake." I went to my office after checking my mailbox in the staff lounge. It was very unusual for me to feel conflicted about telling someone no. And the fact I was spiritually fasting should have certainly made it easy. At times, I had difficulty refusing something depending on my family's or extended family's intimacy level. For some peculiar reason, I struggled with refusing the cake and insulting Mandy.

I juggled between text messaging my husband and answering work emails. "Would it be rude to not celebrate my birthday with them? I am fasting, but I don't want to be rude."

He replied, "Just tell her you don't want the cake."

Asking a co-worker, without telling her I was fasting, I posed the same question. She understood I had requested not to have the cake. "It's your birthday. Just have a nice slice. It will be okay," she replied, thinking it was about the calories. We often spoke of eating healthier and had previously participated in the biggest loser contest as a work-related event.

Throughout the morning, I constantly thought, why did I care about Mandy's feelings like this? If she was rude enough to purchase what I specifically asked her not to, then she deserved my refusal.

I was confident I would not eat the cake until a conversation during lunch with Mandy's friend, Sally. "Mandy bought you a cake. It is not your regular Walmart cake. It is a special cake from an uptown bakery near her house. It's very special." With a grin that must have been the exact grin Satan used to manipulate Eve, Sally casted enough doubt in my mind not to offend Mandy's efforts. Along with Sally's induced doubt, anger resided at my inability to refuse the cake.

Later in the afternoon, a scheduled calendar reminder prompted my attention to my birthday celebration. A phone call followed as I hesitated to go. I prayed for forgiveness for breaking my fast on my way to the school's main office.

When I walked into the main office, someone asked about my procrastination. Mandy decorated on the office corner counter we usually use for celebrations. I read aloud the birthday greeting cards, and the office staff sang the traditional birthday song. During the song, Brock picked up a potted flower Sally purchased for the entire office staff, except me. The recently hired office secretary looked at me as Brock sang and lifted the flower vase up and down. It was apparent he knew about the earlier flower distribution, excluding me by Sally.

Earlier in the morning, shortly after I arrived at the main office, my presence prompted Sally to say she needed to get something. She quickly went to her room and returned with flowers in a small shallow rectangular-shaped box. They were petite flowers in a variety of colored vases. It was usual for us to buy small items for one another or sometimes snacks. As a general unspoken courtesy, we always bought enough for the seven office co-workers.

"Those are beautiful. Where did you get those?" I asked.

Proudly quipping, "Wouldn't you like to know?" Again, regular office play, I assumed. Sally requested the office staff to choose the one each person wanted.

"Let me see which one I want," I said with many assumptions.

"Oh, I didn't buy you one," Sally responded without eye contact. She went to the others to give them their selection.

The office aide looked at me with disappointment seeing I did not realize Sally was not joking. I shrugged it off as it was her money, and she was not obligated to give anything to anyone, including me.

The song ended; Brock put the flower back on the secretary's desk. Mandy opened the clear plastic container to cut the cake. Ladyfinger cookies outlined the circular two-layered Tiramisu cake topped with chocolate shavings. The cake appeared expensive by the well-thought decorating. "See, you like cookies," with a brimming smile and warm-heartedness, Mandy continued, "so I got you a cake with cookies."

In sync with the expectations, I replied, "I see. You did a good job, Mandy."

Loudly repeating my words, Mandy cheerfully announced, "Darline said I did a good job."

I took the knife and sliced in-between the ladyfinger cookies.

"That's all you're getting. It's your birthday, get a larger piece," Mandy encouraged.

With all eyes on me and others waiting, I sliced a bigger slice. I did not know how to respond to peer pressure at the age of fifty, and now, I could not understand. I was not one usually swayed by other folks' feelings and emotions. The desire to maintain a pleasant workplace overrode my judgment. Every neuron in my body screamed, do not!

Taking a couple of bites, I commented the cake was good. It was very moist, almost wet tasting, but it was not a cake I usually ate. Trained by the workplace limited-time lunch's schedule, I defaulted to a fast eater. It was not until I had almost completed the slice before I noticed the sensation starting.

"Why is my throat burning?" I attempted to clear my throat and ate the remainder of the cake. Placing my hand on my chest, I questioned, "Why is my chest burning?"

At my questioning, Sally laughed and ran back and forth between Mandy and me. "Darline said her chest is burning," Sally repeated her words and actions as though she had just witnessed her lifetime's most comical moments.

"What is in this cake?" I asked repeatedly.

The office aide who witnessed the flower incident asked, "Your chest is burning? Maybe you have heartburn."

I tossed my empty plate away. Memories of a similar experience flooded my mind. "No, I remember this feeling. This is not heartburn." Breaking through Sally's laughter, I continued, "Once as a child, I took what I thought was my daddy's Coca-cola, but it was a mixed drink instead. My chest burned just like this." I repeated questioning what was in the cake. It had been over twenty years since I indulged in alcoholic beverages.

Without saying a word about the cake, she purchased, Mandy tossed her plate in the trash. As proud as a losing team's running back who finally reached the end zone, she smiled and walked out of the office with Sally laughing in pursuit.

Sally poked her head back in the office doorway. Like the crackling of thorns under a pot, she stated, "Darline, let me know if you need a ride home."

Brock left and retreated to his office.

Picking up the plastic cake container, I searched the label to see what ingredients were in the cake. The office staff remained and offered to help. The school nurse, visibly upset, affirmed my suspicions. "Darline, you know I drink. And I am telling you the cake has straight rum in it."

The office staff and I continued to look at the label's ingredients. In vain, the office secretary volunteered to call the bakery, San Martin Bakery, in Uptown Dallas, Texas.

The nurse qualified her earlier declaration, "I previously worked in a bakery. That has straight alcohol. It is the strongest alcoholic dessert I have ever had."

"Y'all, Mandy didn't mean to do it," said a sympathizing previous school employee substituting as a data clerk. She was Mandy's long-time work acquaintance. She later offered a mint while commenting on how strong the aftertaste was.

I felt such a strange sensation walking down the hallway to my office with the cake in my hands. I was surprised at the panic in my thoughts of being afraid. I imagined they would further the game by calling the police to tell them I had been drinking once I got in my car after school. It was not only the idea of the alcohol in the cake which made me feel stupid; it was all the spiritual nudging I ignored to spare someone's feelings. Refraining from alcohol was a spiritual commitment.

Not only was I the brunt of deception, but I gave up my fasting to satisfy someone's expectations. It was also the idea Brock and Mandy waited eight months to retaliate against me for making a report to protect children. Their hatred, so profound, led them to ignore any possibility of physical harm.

Embarrassed, I left the main office, returning to my office with the cake in my hands. Private embarrassment will never know the weight of public mockery. I now understood the impact of bullying far better than any textbook or training could teach.

Attempting to resume normalcy by checking my emails, I received an email from Brock, "Can you get drunk from tiramisu cake?" Brock included all the office staff and the school resource officer. I replied, vowing to find out if alcohol was in the cake. I trashed the cake before leaving. Remembering Mandy's words, "Here, take the cake to your family," rallied loudly in my head, indicating she wished to attack my family as well.

I was sure she, Brock, and Sally would have the best of times reliving how I repeatedly asked why my throat and chest burned. Mandy and Brock planned and waited to stick it to this Christian Pastor's wife. Christians who were phony and hypocritical, according to her, but not like me. In her words, she often spoke, "You are the real deal. You calm me." I never believed those comments but never called her out on the behavior as I thought she was just a person who experienced church hurt. Comments about her reasons for not attending church and fake Christians were frequent.

At fifty years old, I fell for something I would have seen five miles ahead if one of my children had told me. Brock, Mandy, and Sally's consistent actions were evidence of their character. Earlier, I refused to accept what Maya Angelo's famous quote, "People show you who they are, believe them."

Feeling defeated, I slowly drove home. What I had just experienced was hatred in its purest form. And I would soon discover this hatred had no intentions in ending. It was not until I made it home when I realized I should have kept the cake.

Chapter 2

The Antecedent

Nothing prepares your mind to see a professional adult allow a young child to invade personal space for gratification. With over twenty years of experience, I never once saw, thankfully, an adult relish in a physical encounter with a child so immensely that the adult did not attempt to separate from the child.

Educators usually respond quickly to detach or remove themselves from children's embraces when needed. We also understand children often need proper social skills and proximity teaching. So, to see Brock, a seasoned educator, freely allow a child to inappropriately touch his genitals was appalling.

Effie struggled with adjusting to classroom routines, as some of the younger students do. I went to Effie's classroom when the teacher could not redirect Effie's behavior and maintain order with the other students. Often removing the student from the environment helps to calm them, so I asked Effie to come with me on a walk to my office. Hand in hand, we easily made it down the hallway, taking a turn towards my office near the cafeteria. Brock walked out of the cafeteria, and Effie ran and latched herself around Brock's lower body.

It was not the hugging motion, as it is common for children to grab hold of adults. By his voice inflections and startling movements, Brock knew Effie touched him in a sensitive area. Brock's inaudible sounds acknowledged her touch. Instead of

Brock making any attempts to remove himself or Effie, he smiled and repeated several times, "Yes, the shirt is blue." Hypnotized by the blue shirt comment and his inaction, I froze in uncertainty. Realizing the interaction would continue, I went and removed Effie from Brock. Not missing a beat, Brock smiled as he strolled down the hallway.

While still in a daze, I paused when a teacher called my name and requested to talk with me. I was able to keep my composure. Focusing as best as possible, I could not remove the incident's image while the teacher discussed her concerns. Effie wandered in the hallway, and the teacher demanded her back where we stood. I saw the child's behavior but could not reprimand her.

Before school's dismissal, I went to Brock's office with Mandy to debrief about the day. Offhandedly, Brock mentioned how Effie grabbed his leg. Awkwardly clamping his teeth to create a smile after his statement alarmed me as deception and manipulation. I then knew what I witnessed was not a figment of my imagination. Brock's attempt to alter the incident without prompting gave more assurance. I decided to call Child Protective Services as soon as I arrived home.

Once I got home, I prepared dinner and prayed. The anxiety of another poor relationship with my supervisor rose within me. I wondered how in the world did I manage to get caught up in such foolishness. I prayed for my strength and for those in charge to do what was right by the child.

Later in the evening, I called Child Protective Services to report the incident. Afterwards, I emailed the counseling department director and copied the superintendent. I did not think twice about reporting Brock to Child Protective Services or the district. I felt emotionally numbed until the phone rang. It was not a contact number on my cell phone, so I answered assuming it was the counseling department director. I prepared to talk with her, but not the district's superintendent, Mr. Glazier.

He introduced himself and asked me to give him the specifics. Mr. Glazier reaffirmed my actions in the conversation periodically, stating, "You did the right thing." Although I did not need the approval, those words later became a soothing salve in the days to come. However, at the moment, my actions to call and report the principal were the least of my concern. The decision to call Child Protective Services occurred earlier in the afternoon without any reservation.

After giving him the details and letting him know I called Child Protective Services, I asked, "So, do I return to work tomorrow?" It was a more loaded question than I realized and one which brought a flood of painful memories. A question that was the release of suppressed emotions and exposed the need for healing. A question that was probably the dumbest question to ask a superintendent of a school district.

With a surprised tone, "Yes, you go back as normal."

The silence permeated the entire room.

"Hello. Are you okay?"

Choking back tears and pausing, I forced out, "Just a moment."

"Are you okay?"

Sitting on my bed's edge in silence, I prayed to God. *Please do not let me cry to this man, the district's superintendent!*

Yes, I had included him in the email. Still, I had not expected him to call. What superintendent of a large district calls employees who send an email? Certainly, he receives an overload of daily emails. I just wanted him to be aware of the report. I hoped he would see to proper procedures and measures did not fall through the broken and sometimes careless system.

Being in this district for eight years with previous experiences, I knew how easily things could go unchecked. I wanted to make sure the repulsive incident did not get swept under the rug. But here I was on the phone, trying to sound professional and not like a traumatized adult who should have been on the phone with a professional counselor.

Mr. Glazier broke the silence, inferring my hesitancy, "We don't do retaliation in this district."

Pulled by his declaration of no retaliation, the memories of my previous school's leadership flooded. Like a river's dam broken after a level ten hurricane, my words released, "This district is horrible!"

Diplomatically, he inquired, "Why do you say that?"

My mind and mouth rebirthed every memory of my previous school's experience in the same district. I told him about the racism I experienced, and the former and present people involved, who were there, and not there presently. In a split second, I continued explaining frequent meetings, the emails between the previous administration and me, how someone looked, and everything my mouth caught from my mind. I might as well have told him what color clothing everyone wore each day.

After I paused for air, I projected more, "And I still have all my documentation. I even have the letter from the former area director stating the need for new practices regarding racism with the school's principal who is still there."

He probed a little more about my administrators, "Are your current supervisors treating you okay?"

"Yes. I know I cannot base the present from the past. Brock and Mandy have been kind," I replied, referring to the previous year. It was the beginning of the second year with Brock, and I knew things were about to change. I feared Brock would not see this as doing my legal and moral obligation. Brock enjoyed the power which came with his position as someone who once may have felt helpless.

26

"Okay, we will just move forward. As I said, we don't retaliate."

Thinking all the flooding was over, my mind reacted to the word retaliation again. "Well, that's what happened to Mr. Rosario."

"Who?"

"Mr. Rosario," I repeated.

"What about him?"

I felt obligated to tell him. Something needed to be done quickly because I knew my work environment and relationship with Brock would take a nosedive. Brock needed to understand his behavior was unacceptable. Children were at risk in his care.

I quickly reflected on the afternoon's conversation with Brock and Mandy. Though I believed I kept my composure, it was apparent Brock tried to reinvent the story. Brock did not realize bringing up the conversation unprovoked, and explaining the incident, confirmed my beliefs. I also knew what Mr. Rosario reported, but it was not until now I completely believed his encounters with Brock.

I continued by explaining Mr. Rosario's report about Brock's arousal from staring at a student as Mr. Rosario and Brock waited for late parents. "Mr. Rosario reported him last year. Brock picked on Mr. Rosario and gave him an unsatisfactory evaluation. Realizing this was supposed to be confidential information, and Mr. Rosario was not the one who told me, I quickly added, "Another co-worker told me."

Superintendents apparently have enough experience to maintain a poker persona. Even at this, he simply stated, "I will have someone to call you tonight. Tell the person who calls you that allegedly Brock had a previous incident. He then inquired, "Is there anything Brock has done that makes you think this is his character?"

"Yes. In two different meetings with parents and two additional staff members, Brock referred to third-grade students as virgin test-takers because they had never done it before, referring to the state tests."

"He said what?" Mr. Glazier chuckled in disbelief. Continuing, he asked, "he said that in front of the parents?" That was the only time in the conversation the superintendent's voice had any emotional inflection.

"Yes, I asked Mandy's opinion about it because I know sometimes, I can be a little square. She said it was inappropriate, and I should have called him out on it."

"No, you did the right thing. You shouldn't have called him out on it." Returning to his initial composure, "If no one calls you tonight, then call me back. Okay?"

My bedroom absorbed the tornado of emotions. As a child to a caring parent, released from anxiety, "Okay."

Emotionally drained, I went into the living room and plopped on the sofa beside my husband. With reddish eyes, smeared mascara, and a flushed face, I announced, "Well, I guess I won't have a job soon, and I feel like a fool."

"You sure have been in the room for a long time," he replied.

"I freaking cried to the superintendent!"

Turning completely from the television, he asked, "To who?"

"The superintendent."

"Of what?"

"The school district."

"How did you get on the phone with him?"

I explained after I contacted Child Protective Services, I sent an email to my director because I did not have her phone number. I carbon copied him because I knew sometimes the proper chain of command could be broken. To leave children exposed to someone who may be a predator was unacceptable.

"How did he respond during the call?"

"Well, there was only one time his voice revealed emotions. It was Brock's reference to third graders being virgin test-takers."

The phone call from the superintendent arrested my husband's attention. "I just cannot believe a superintendent of this size district would call an employee! They normally would have someone else do that."

While my husband's focus remained captured on the superintendent's response to the email, I pondered over my reaction at the superintendent if I saw him in the district soon. I cried profusely. And I took him back years concerning my former principal from previous years.

Emotionally strained for the last five years I did not realize I was experiencing post-traumatic stress, even as a counselor. It was my professional counseling supervisor during an internship session who identified the trauma for me. I occupied my mind with busyness trying not to allow the past to creep into my present decision-making. Fighting against insecurities, I was determined to hold my head up despite the previous supervisor's evilness.

While taking care of those depending on me at work, home, and church ministries, I suppressed feelings. I tucked them away as I did not have the time or desire to deal with the previous school principal's harassment aftermath. As with our health, it will finally make us take care of ourselves. My emotional lid fully opened, and there was no force to restrain the release.

"Well, what else did he say? You were in the room for a long time!"

"I told him Mandy said I should have questioned or called out Brock when he referred to the third-grade students as virgin

29

test takers. Mr. Glazier encouraged that I did right not to call him out on it."

Having difficult supervisors' experiences, my husband agreed with the superintendent. He then asked, "Why do you think you won't have a job?

"After trying not to cry and regain composure, I just blurted out the entire district was horrible. Who tells the boss of all bosses the company is horrible?"

He hopefully responded, "Obviously, God knew you needed to get all of that out. It all happened for a reason. I wouldn't worry about your job. Districts have protocols in place for these kinds of things. Man, I can't believe the superintendent called!"

I realized my husband was not going to get past this now. It must have been very unusual. As a former school principal, I assumed he knew the likelihood of upper-level administrators having the time to call employees. Curious, he asked, "Why did you ask the superintendent about returning to work?"

Flinging my hands in the air, I confessed, "I don't know!"

My cell phone interrupted our conversation. It was the district's investigator, Janie Lang, charismatic and personable. She asked me to recall the details and give her the building's location where the incident occurred. Then she asked to describe the clothing I had on during the time of the incident. The conversation did not last long, which I needed, quick, and to the point.

Later in the same bedroom which bored my emotional release's burden became a prayer sanctuary. My husband prayed with me. I just did not want to have another year of tension with administrators. He assured me Brock more than likely would not be in the building and not to worry. Proper protocol removes an employee until after the investigation. If nothing is substantiated, he will return.

As a teacher, it is common to have mixed feelings about new leadership; it comes with the territory. People often assume things can be done better regarding leaders. We do not see the broad perspective of how our choices or decisions impact a system. We usually center leaderships' choices and decisions on how it affects us.

However, I could not take the same approach to this tension as I did with the previous school's leadership. The elementary school counselor's position is considered the third administrator. The last thing I wanted was the obligation of working as part of the administrative team without trust.

It was the beginning of the school year, and I did not desire a troublesome year with Brock. In Brock's first year at the school, he appeared to be trying too hard to fit in and make an impression. I viewed Brock as socially awkward, with no intent to harm. His frequent remarks about marriage led me to believe he did not have a social outlet within his marriage or friendships. The number of times he discussed his marital disconnection was uncomfortable. I offered no counsel to maintain a boundary.

Attempting not to be too judgmental, I ignored his seemingly quirks, despite my husband's warnings to go with what I felt. After witnessing his behavior in the hallway with Effie, I detested everything about Brock.

Before long, I confided in Mandy about his constant comments about his marriage. I did not know Brock and preferred not to discuss with a man his marital concerns. Mandy claimed to have noticed, as well. When the comments stopped, I did not consider she might tell him as she greatly pretended to hate Brock. I eventually saw Mandy's true character as she conspired with Brock in mistreating staff members.

As my husband turned over in bed, and I prepared to get in, he was still in awe of the superintendent's phone call. "I just can't believe the superintendent of this district's size would call you. You should have gotten me a job!"

We both laughed at his comment, but it was the last laugh concerning this incident we shared.

Chapter 3

Take Care of Yourself

Simultaneously, Brock and I approach the workday with caution when we saw each other the next morning. The moment I saw him walk past my office, without a doubt, I knew someone informed Brock of my report. Without speaking, his worried expression demonstrated we were now in a strained relationship. He walked so far on the opposite side of the hall his shirt stroked against the wall.

After I settled in my office, my counseling director came unexpectedly. When directors or upper administration came to school buildings unannounced, it signaled a concern or problem. I presumed the counseling director came to discuss my CPS report.

Walking in my office, she mentioned that the superintendent called before her visit regarding my conversation with him. I often stood amazed at her delayed aging beautiful, dark-skin, and classiness. She was maybe in her early to mid-seventies. Stoically, she explained she was at church and did not check emails once she arrived home. I gave her the incident's repulsive details, which required the CPS report. I hoped she would advocate and support.

The director interjected to ask what the blue shirt comment meant. I told her I had no idea. After listening, she respectfully questioned, "I have to ask. What made you carbon copied the superintendent?"

I felt horrible I had spoken with the superintendent before speaking with her, although it was not my intention. The rumor of her job being in jeopardy floated throughout the district. I did not have the heart to say I wanted to make sure this was dealt with and not lost in the chain of command. With over forty years in the district, upper-level administration sense of urgency can change as their ears appear dull to campus-level employees.

Reflections of Brock smiling as the child touched him and the blue shirt comments paused my response. I re-engaged in the conversation. "I didn't expect the superintendent to call. I didn't have your number, so I did what I thought was the next best thing."

Placing her hand on her chest, impeccably dressed and well-poised as usual, she stated, "I have been in this position a long time. I have never had anyone to include a superintendent in an email to me." She proceeded, informing the district had protocols in place.

I understood her concern. It may have appeared I disrespected her position. However, my purpose was to protect children. I resolved I could not mishandle the responsibility regardless of protocols and feelings.

The counselor director stood to leave, slightly glancing around the office. Before departing, she casually warned, "Well, take care of yourself until they get him out of here. Principals are known to retaliate."

Surprised by her response but not the warning, I resisted commenting she was preaching to the choir. I could have written a book on the Rope-a- Dope, Bob and Weave, using my previous school's experience. I spent almost five years under leadership that would have been better if a young child were in control. Children respond more to actions than skin color.

A few months after our conversation, her demotion from department director to a middle school counselor spread throughout the district. It was the most disrespectful demotion I ever witnessed in education, especially when the consequences of Brock's behavior and the others involved were comfortable and secured rewards. White privilege is equally as real as racism. I did not know the reason for her demotion. However, it was not inappropriate behavior with a student or workplace harassment for certainty.

Shortly after the counseling director left, I exchanged emails with Janie Lang about the timestamp for the video recordings located in the hallway. After a few email exchanges, Janie Lang responded that she located the video footage and asked for a written statement of the incident.

For a few weeks, Brock and I did not greet each other or spoke only if necessary. He stood in my doorway, partially in the hallway, before Student Support Team meetings until someone else came in. Once while we were waiting for the next meeting, a young second-grade girl came to speak and hug him; he pushed her away in panic. I understood his reaction. If accused of inappropriate behavior with a child, I would have taken precautions as well.

A few days later, a Child Protective Service investigator came to my office. As a school counselor, I frequently met with CPS investigators. When I realized she was there regarding the report concerning Effie, I panicked.

Whispering in my closed office, "I didn't think you would come here!"

Perplexed, she responded, "Yes, I have to investigate and talk with the child."

"No, my principal is here!" My response confused her even more as she looked at her report. Of course, from her perspective, the principal would be in the school building. Seeing she was not understanding, I continued to whisper, "He's the perpetrator."

"Oh, I didn't know that," she paused, "this report does not state that, but I have to speak to the child."

"No! You can't. She's only five, and you can't understand her. I don't even know if the parents know." Effie struggled to express herself. Very few words she spoke were understandable as she mumbled especially to unfamiliar adults. I knew putting Effie in that situation would cause more harm than good.

"Oh, I have to inform the parents."

"I understand. I'm just saying I don't know if the parents are aware yet." No one from the district followed up with me. Since Brock remained on the campus, I had no way of knowing the direction of the investigation. I went to my computer and wrote down the district's investigator's name with the email address. I also printed the written statement I gave to the investigator.

After reading my written statement, the CPS worker, surprised with the clarity, stated that she had received the wrong information in her report. Without asking to speak to the student again and ensuring I would later hear from her, she left.

Because the CPS worker did not understand that Brock was the perpetrator, I called CPS again the following Saturday morning. I explained to the intake person my concerns. She assured me I was overthinking, and the information in her files was correct, as I reported.

However, I witnessed the CPS investigator did not have accurate information. I realized the person on the phone did not appear to have any concerns that the information was incorrect. I reasoned perhaps the report was not read correctly before the visit with me. CPS is an overwhelmed system, and with a high turnover rate, mistakes can happen.

In staff meetings, Brock often reminded the staff in tricky situations, "smile and nod." This saying became my daily mantra as I entered the building. The workplace atmosphere was daunting. I could not confide in anyone, just smile and pretend.

The worst stress I felt was Brock's presence around children. If I saw him with a child or escorting a child to his office, my heart raced. Sometimes I went into the office and just stood there near the secretary's desk. Because I did not want to ruin his reputation without a complete investigation, I kept it confidential for a while, thinking the district worked to remove Brock.

Later within the next month, Janie Lang came to the school one afternoon to administer a climate survey. It was the only time I heard anything of or from her after the CPS report. Before she spoke, Brock explained to the staff it was just an administrative checkpoint like what he had to do with teachers. As the staff sat at the cafeteria's tables, we wondered the true reason for the recently announced meeting. After making a joke about not being able to participate, Brock left.

Although Brock did not introduce Janie's title, some of the staff knew her role as it was not the first time coming since Brock was appointed. Janie Lang investigated Mr. Rosario's report of Brock's inappropriate behavior during Brock's first year. She interviewed several people from the school regarding Mr. Rosario's concern.

Janie Lang explained the survey and the reasons she came in person. Many people did not feel electronic reviews were confidential from her experiences, so she came to give a paper copy. A couple of teachers asked questions and expressed concerns about administrators' bullying behaviors.

The staff trickled out as each one completed the survey. I left without eye contact with Janie Lang, not wanting anyone to think I was the one who had contact with her. It was crazy to think anyone could have known just from eye contact. However, a survey instead of a follow-up report regarding Brock caused many confusing moments. As usual, the staff did not receive any results from the survey.

A week or two later, Effie's teacher stopped me in the hallway, curious about why the parents approached her about Child Protective Services. It was apparent the teacher was unaware. The parents not having the right information was also evident. The parents would not have questioned the teacher if they knew what the report stated. No district personnel must have explained the concerns to them. I acted indifferently, still assuming the district was attempting to investigate. The teacher walked with her kinder class, so it was easy to break away as she managed the students.

The weeks went on, and it was business as usual. Brock continued buying lunch for the office staff, which I always refused after Effie's incident. The office staff noticed. Once, the office secretary pleaded with me to get lunch since he continued to offer. She had a soft spot for Brock, although I did not understand why she wanted my participation. I attempted the usual spill; I wanted to eat the food I brought from home. Mandy heard me refusing one day and stated, "She doesn't want anything from Brock!" Since I had not disclosed Brock's behavior with the child to Mandy, I ordered.

Mandy had previously asked what was up between Brock and me. At the time, I believed it was a sincere question from her observations. I avoided answering the questions since I was left in the dark about the CPS report's investigation. I did not want to give unconfirmed information.

Sitting beside him in the faculty break area, I slowly nibbled at the Jimmy John's sandwich. The fact Brock bought it changed the sandwich's taste, although this was one of my favorite cold sandwich shops. The atmosphere was thick from the silence between Brock and me. It was the last time I agreed to eat anything purchased by him.

Chapter 4

Working from Memories

Around October, I realized I should attempt to protect my evaluation. It is prevalent for school administrators to release administrative tasks to counselors. School counselors struggle to provide much-needed services for students. Students wait for days to see counselors as we balance the required paperwork from various state- mandated programs.

In addition to the paperwork, parent meetings for mandatory documentation consume a lot of a counselor's time. The only situation that abrupt a counselor's schedule immediately is a suicide threat or administrators' requests to assist with students. However, most administrators did not hold counselors responsible for deficiencies resulting from extra administrative duties.

Recalling Brock's retaliatory behaviors with Mr. Rosario prompted a proactive stance for my counseling performance review. Brock was the responsible supervisor. It was preposterous the district, having full knowledge of my CPS report, would still have Brock as my evaluator.

I also recalled the beginning of the school year when Mandy informed me of who my evaluator was. Leaving her office one morning, she called me back. "Hey, just a heads up. Brock is your evaluator this year." Mandy's attitude when she shared Brock was my evaluator indicated concern, but I did not initially jump to conclusions.

Remembering I walked this path before with supervisors, I decided to intercept the play. I sent an email to the counseling department's director. I included Brock and Mandy, as I addressed my concerns about having additional responsibilities outside of the counselor's scope. After continuous pressure from Mandy, Brock gave an extra testing assignment to manage. Sending the email was my way of safeguarding my evaluation from Brock's possible attempts in sabotaging it. In the email, I expressed concerns about the new duties given but planned to comply with the tasks assigned. I indicated I might not be able to satisfy the rubric and expectations of the counseling program.

The counseling department's director did not respond, but Brock assured her he would work with me. My little stunt resulted in weekly meetings with Brock to discuss updates on my workload. I did not want to see Brock more than I needed. The disingenuous conversations between us were grueling. Occasionally, Brock invited Mandy, which made it worse. Entertaining one was more than enough.

Manipulative supervisors were of the many situations I referred to during the superintendent's call which led me to say the district was horrible. Within the same district, three years prior, I defended my evaluation when accused of being abrasive towards students. Paula, the school's principal, used her assistants as henchmen.

Paula, for an unknown reason, did not like me. Rumors from her clique insisted if she did not like you, she would never like you. Paula chased for the bullseye from my first year at the school. She and the previous principal stopped the frequent meetings after I emailed requesting to meet with all the concerned parents they claimed called.

Since Paula and I seldom interacted, I suspected it was a racial issue. Still, I did not want to believe my skin color was her motivation. Perhaps Paula was not a qualified leader whose lack of interpersonal skills became a barrier to building positive relationships. After all, her entire office staff quit, except for one person, after Paula's promotion to the school's principal. Eventually, the remaining staff clerk left after pleading for another placement.

In Paula's first year as principal, I felt something was brewing. One of my co-workers, a long-standing clique member of Paula's, stated that Claudia, the assistant principal, graded very hard on evaluations. I was not concern about the grading expectations. My previous fifteen career evaluations ranged from proficient to exemplary.

Claudia had recently transferred to our school. The former employees knew her in the role of an instructional coach. There was no way of knowing how Claudia evaluated since she had not been in the role or position to evaluate using the state's appraisal system.

Before the end of the year evaluation meeting, there were many conferences with Paula and Claudia. Student relationships were always the administrators' targeted area, as it is a prerequisite for any counseling career. Rehearsed and familiar lines were my sixth-grade students reported I acted as though I did not want to work or an unusual number of parents called regarding my sluggish countenance. If the parents were not calling, Paula needed me to look happier and act more enthused, especially for the sixth grade "babies" as she called them.

One of the many summoned meetings with Paula and Claudia, I sat sombrely waiting for the usual conversations. Paula started by stating, "I know you stayed home for three years with your son. It can be difficult returning to work.". Every meeting with Paula included the reference to the time I was a stay home mom. Paula looked at her notes to address her newest claim. "Darline, a student reported that you are constantly getting into his business."

Stunned by Paula's comment, I asked her to explain. This was a new kind of accusation from Paula. Usually, her concerns were with how I interacted with the honors classes who were mostly White. Regular classes rarely received concerns. The student she referenced was a Black child who had tardiness problems and sleeping in class most days.

I recalled talking with the student and asking him why he could not stay awake in class. I asked him to come into the hallway to speak with me. His reason was the family had returned from Louisiana from the weekend. And without sleep or breakfast, he came to school. I went to the cafeteria to get something for the student to eat while a neighboring teacher talked with him. The student and I had a very normal conversation and relationship.

After explaining the conversation with the student to Paula, she responded, "Well, he feels uncomfortable in your class."

Confused, I attempted to reason what could have gone wrong until Paula smirked. I recalled the neighboring teacher, who spoke with the student, was Paula's good friend. Paula accomplished her goal, creating doubt and frustration. I ended the meeting in my usual way by saying I would reflect on their concerns. Batting back tears, I wanted to snatch Paula like a wet Raggedy Ann doll from across her desk. Most people do not realize the blessings of tears. Some believe tears indicate victory, not understanding tears are grace.

Attempting to maintain positive interactions, I accepted the responsibility of resolving the pseudo-problems the best way possible. In my past experiences, the way you approached reciprocated the same actions from me. However, I wanted to rise above the Enemies' tactics and be a more diligent witness for Christ. Paula threw every dart she thought from her wicked mind.

After two years of Paula's privilege to demean, insult, and waste my time as I pretended to be unaware of her schemes, I decided it was enough. Paula was now at the "one more time" level. I desired to communicate with others when emotionally upset without disrespecting them and God. I prayed for God to give me the wisdom and calmness I needed. I remembered a good friend's counsel to learn to play the game. Be calm, be direct, and pretend as if nothing happened the next day. A White principal mentor shared this advice to assist her with maintaining good working relationships in the district.

In another meeting, entering her office, I looked at the standard set up, Paula, behind her desk, and Claudia nearby. Before directing any comments towards me, Paula turned to Claudia and told her I was a stay-at-home mom for three years before coming to the school. They began the conversation by informing me a co-worker complained I yelled too much and disturbed classrooms around me.

I asked Paula for the co-worker to join the meeting. I received the usual response from Paula. "The co-worker is afraid of you."

I reminded Paula of my previous request for professional courtesy to speak with concerned people as she allowed other staff, especially her friends.

Paula defaulted to the normal response, "Parents and your colleagues fear retaliation from you."

Claudia chimed in, "Darline, if you are getting the same complaints as you did last year, then maybe you need to consider it is you."

I was aware Claudia, recently returning to the school, might not have known Paula's true intentions. However, she decided to take a shot, and I decided to catch the rebound. "People say many things about a lot of people. You should know that." Claudia shifted in her seat, indicating she inferred she was the topic of many conversations. I continued, "If you ask me if I raise my voice, I will admit in situations when students are too loud, and I need to get their attention. Screaming, no."

I could have accepted the criticism had it been true. However, being a part of an environment allows you to know the environment's inner workings.

Paula attempted to back Claudia's statements, "Darline, I have to admit I passed by your classroom once, and I heard you screaming."

It was a well-known fact Paula seldom left her desk for fear of not having her Dr. Pepper to sip. I knew the possibility of her leaving her office was minuscule. Leaning in towards her desk with direct eye contact, I retorted, "If you heard me screaming, then you should have checked on me. Maybe I had lost my mind." I felt my emotions rising on the Richter scale. The memory of my friend's voice reminded me not to give them what they wanted, an angry Black woman.

Paula's snicker confirmed my friend's counsel and subdued my desire to express frustration. Releasing shoulders, I relaxed backward in the chair. I admonished Paula that it was very unprofessional to have children remain in an emotionally abusive environment. As leaders, it was their responsibility to protect children. I questioned Paula about why she did not spend any time in my classrooms if she received numerous complaints.

Paula agreed her visibility was inadequate but continued with her agenda. They gave me a list of expectations. I wrote the notes , knowing some were against policy, individualized mistreatment, and position abuse. They documented the meeting and asked for my signature as an acknowledgment of our conversation. I signed the first letter without a counter-response.

Later, I received an email to sign a second letter. Claudia's email stated the first letter did not have the school's letterhead. Figuring this was an attempt to elicit emotions, I signed the second one with the letterhead and returned it to Claudia. I knew the letter had no merit. Later, Claudia came twice to my classroom; Paula did not. Claudia's observations were without follow-up reports or debriefing.

When it was time for my yearly post-conference, they thought the letter was enough to use against my teacher's evaluation. True to my expectations, Claudia wrote a negative comment concerning student relationships. I refused to sign the evaluation because it referred to me as abrasive towards students. I also explained that legally hearsay could not be included in an evaluation to which Claudia agreed.

It was time for my students to return to class, so Claudia walked with me to continue the conversation. Claudia assured me she was not trying to hurt my future goal of becoming a school counselor. We decided to meet again after she considered her wording on the evaluation. The conversation was pleasant. I was proud, thinking I had managed a resolution in a way we could appreciate, respectfully and productively.

Not even a week later, I was proven wrong. On a Friday afternoon, Claudia scheduled an after-school meeting. Twisting the knife, she changed abrasive to a synonym expecting me to sign the documents.

"No, I am not signing an evaluation that includes hearsay and not your observations."

Annoyed, Claudia responded, "You signed the letter earlier this year, acknowledging our conversation on student and staff relationships."

"Exactly. Acknowledging the meeting. What you are doing is against policy."

Claudia decided to get Paula. While waiting on both, I prayed, asking God for a better way. I did not want to use what I heard from a trusted source.

Claudia returned to the office with Paula, who looked as though she had won her favorite prize. Paula sat in a chair beside me, and Claudia returned behind her desk. Knowing fully of the problem, Paula asked, "Darline, tell me why you won't sign the evaluation?"

I had a quick nonspiritual vision: *Right hook, left uppercut, and push kick. Paula falls backward through the wall.* Feeding into her ego, I went over my concerns. Then they both repeated what I prayed they would not. Paula stated, "Well, we believe you did it. No, we didn't hear you, but we believe you were abrasive towards students."

Claudia supported, "Yes, I believe it as well!"

Leaving the chair I sat in, I stood in the doorway. I did not trust to be in the office with them. I released the ammunition in slow cadence, "I have asked you both to stop telling me what you heard. Since you want to tell me what you heard and how you believe it, let me tell you what I heard. Claudia, I heard you curse the kids out. Do you want me to call them in one by one and see what each one says? I do not curse adults and surely would not curse a student. Should I believe what I heard?"

Startled eyes and speechless, she froze. I allowed the words to linger a moment. Another nonspiritual vision occurred: *With my finger in her face, "Oh, you don't have anything to say? Choking on what I heard, uh?"*

Turning towards Paula, "Paula, I heard you make sure people you dislike receive a poor evaluation. Should I believe what I heard?"

The nonspiritual visions were at an all-time high: In full-body motions of right and left hooks, each punch having its word, *You coward! You really make me sick. You are the worst leader ever! We all dislike you."*

Without responding to the accusations, Paula asked, "Darline, what can we do to get you to sign the evaluation?"

I requested, "You will give me a copy of the evaluation with the word abrasive. Change it, and then give me a clean copy to sign." Though I was angry, I knew to keep receipts. A nonspiritual vision caused me to pause. *And while you're at it, kiss my what I heard behind!*

Happy to have an exit, Paula ran out to make a copy. There was so much fire in me with no way to extinguish it. When Claudia asked for my social security number to make the change, I told her to get it the best way possible or the way she got it the first time. Then I proceeded to discuss my disappointment with her behavior.

Claudia tried to respond, "That's your opinion."

I interrupted her mid-sentence, letting her know she attempted to hold me to a standard she did not exhibit. And she was legally out of the timeline for evaluations. Claudia ignored my statements, typing on the computer to make the changes to my evaluation.

From prize-winner to frayed, Paula returned with copies of the first evaluation by the time Claudia printed the second. I signed the second copy. I left Claudia's office and told my daughter, who was in the main office area waiting for me to get her things.

It was not a victory nor satisfying. I did not want this kind of interaction or environment. For once in my life, I sincerely attempted to take a different approach in communicating with others. I just wanted to go to work, do my job, and go home. I felt the more I tried, the more I was being hindered.

Shortly after leaving, the Black teachers texted as they knew about the meeting. It was standard practice to attempt to discourage Black teachers at the school. I should have left the school after this incident, but that was Paula's goal. My spiritual goal was to stop running in the face of adversity. I did not think I was going to accomplish this as I desperately contemplated quitting that evening.

Although Claudia had this experience with me, she continued along the same path. A few weeks later, I assisted another Black teacher, who was also their target the teacher's first year. After being reported to human resources, Claudia's directive was to apologize to the teacher and void her evaluation. In good timing, the teacher received a promotion to another school at the end of the school year.

The following school year, Claudia was supportive and kind. Her behavior indicated she realized how Paula operated with specific teachers or I would not play the game. I did not allow her previous behavior to hinder our working relationship. She had a choice not to permit Paula to dictate her actions, but her behavior change towards me was enough. Claudia requested to return to her previous school as an assistant principal at the end of her second year. One of the principal's good friends, Denise, became the new assistant.

Denise was previously a teacher and department leader in our school. Along with a few others, I was not happy about her return. Paula shot arrows through Denise as well. As a department leader and co-worker, Denise often came to harass me.

Once, after completing my attendance, I got up from the computer prepared to begin the lesson. Sitting in the back of my class unannounced, was Denise. Because I previously had several incidents with Denise and Paula, I knew Denise's presence signaled Paula's arrow shot. Walking to the student's desk where she sat, I questioned, "Why are you here?"

She responded, "I'm just here."

Knowing my daughter had Denise's class during the same period, covered by a student-teacher alone, this was another "let's break her plan." I posed another question seeking clarity. "Are you observing me?"

Uncomfortably quick, she chirped, "No, I'm just here."

Annoyed and confused, I went on to teach my students.

That evening, I decided to address the situation directly. After arriving home, I emailed the principals, including Denise. I directly asked why Denise observed me. She was a teacher without administrative rights for unannounced observations. I stated that I would not allow her to bully me and requested a meeting with Denise. Paula rarely responded to emails, so Claudia did. Claudia indicated Denise came to my classroom as a collaboration plan within the department.

Denise and I had a worthless meeting about her goals as department leader. In the meeting, I addressed the teacher next to me was new to the district. I had frequent observations, whereas the new teacher had none nor the assistance she desired. Denise claimed she was doing something new in the department. The following week, she observed the teacher next to me but did not observe the others in our department for the entire school year.

Denise did not take long to repeat high surveillance tactics in her new role, assistant principal. She raised the stakes by soliciting other district department personnel to come into my classroom, claiming I needed more engaging lessons for the honors students. Honors-level students were most often district personnel and well-known, active parents' children. These classes would have mostly White students. The students placed in my regular course were predominantly Black and Hispanic students, so I did not need help teaching them. I ducked and dodged their attempts and received a proficient evaluation.

In Denise's second year, she increased everything she had done previously. She also suggested that I needed to visit another school to see quality classroom instruction for honors students. It was apparent her behavior was personal and not professional. Many co-workers in my department knew and were simply confused at the constant dog tracking behaviors.

Denise requested another meeting. Once again, concerned and nameless parents were one of the issues. This time the parents stated the students were "afraid" to attend tutorials. I maintained detailed tutorial logs, which were several pages. However, Denise never asked to see them. I did not offer, knowing it would not have mattered.

In the written follow-up, she also included I did not address students by name per her observation in my class. With at least one-hundred and twenty students, I did not always recall names. I sometimes called the children I carried nine months and birthed a different name. With the constant pressure from Paula's foolishness, the goal was survival, not the memory game.

When I came from Denise's office, a group of department co-workers was in the hall. Frustrated, I asked all of them to read the letter I had received from Denise. One of the White teachers laughed loudly, "This is not even our school's correct letterhead!"

"Darline, you know what this is, right?" questioned another teacher.

"What? Stupidity?"

"This is racism," she informed.

It is one thing to suspect and discuss possible racism with other Blacks. But when you have a White person opening your eyes to racism, it adds confirmation you are not playing the race card. You are the bait for personal pleasures. I walked away, disgusted and wanting to quit.

My prayer life grew as I needed strength to restrain from violent actions or words with Denise and Paula. It was a time of spiritual maturity I, at times, attempted to rebel against the growth.

Once I was spiritually inclined to respond differently to Denise and Paula. I went to grab breakfast tacos at Taco Cabana one morning. After eating two in the car and content, I pulled out of my parking space to head to the school. I did not make it out of the parking lot as I felt the Holy Spirit prompting me to purchase a dozen variety tacos for the administrators. I argued with God before being obedient.

Driving my car back into a parking space, I questioned God's prompting. *Are you kidding me? You want me to spend my money on ole evil Paula and Denise?* The scripture from Proverbs 25:22 (ESV) came to mind, "If your enemy is hungry, give him bread to eat, and if he is thirsty, give him water to drink, for you will heap burning coals on his head, and the Lord will reward you." However, it did not comfort me. I did not care about coals or rewards. Paula would see my efforts of kindness as a weakness. I explained to God if I purchased the tacos, Paula would send Denise into my room that day to prove her feelings towards me. I pleaded, "*God, buying tacos is pulling Paula's chain!*"

Reluctantly, I carried the box into the office and handed it to Sam, an assistant principal, who thanked me. Paula came from her office upon hearing me talk to Sam, smiled warmly, and expressed gratitude. I smiled and engaged in a little small talk. Paula's eyes and smile were incongruent. If I could only figure out why this woman hated me, I would label myself a genius.

By the afternoon, Denise came into my classroom for observation on a partial school day. I am sure God laughed when I said, "*I told you, so!*" Every teacher in America knows it was not a good sign or purpose when an administrator came into your classroom on a partial school day. Students are known to be at their wildest on partial school days and days before holidays.

Knowing the reason for Denise's observation, I allowed her presence to stir my emotions. I became agitated with the students while teaching the lesson. I walked several times by Denise, glaring down at what she wrote on her yellow legal paper. Each time I passed by, I had unspiritual visions of snatching the pen and scribbling on her face. She later emailed me for another meeting in her office.

I went into the office on the requested day and time with Denise and Sam. It was well-known by the staff Paula just dictated the moves but stayed clear of any confrontations. I was not surprised by Paula's absence. Again, I took my notepad for documentation. I prayed. This time I decided I would not say one word unless asked a question, but my plans plummeted quickly.

Denise talked behind her desk while Sam sat against the wall facing me. She opened the conversation by saying it was just a conversation, and there was no reason for concern. Denise stated the issues of how I appeared annoyed and stressed with the students. I told her the observations were correct and her frequent visits were the reason I was agitated. Sam chimed in about observations were common. I believed Sam was unaware of the frequency and reasons for mine. I did not address him.

I addressed Denise others in my department had not had one walkthrough, nor had she visited the new teachers. Denise acknowledged and noted she was going to make other teachers' observations soon.

The conversation took a turn for the worse when Denise played the broken record. Twirling a pen between her fingers, she leaned slightly as with authority and quipped, "Darline, I know you have a great relationship with the staff. Everyone likes you. You all have fun together. But you have got to learn how to have good relationships with the students." Sounding very emphatically, she continued, "You have a counseling degree, so I'm sure you can do it. I know you don't like the school…"

My plan of not responding to accusations became a memory. Looking directly at Denise, calmly and firmly, I interrupted, "Let me stop you. I like the school. I live five to ten minutes from here in good traffic. I like the school. I like the staff. I don't like you. I don't trust you. I don't like Paula. I don't trust Paula, and you can go tell her that."

When Sam chuckled unintentionally, I realized he was still there. Denise attempted to recover from these statements quickly. "Well, I don't want you not to trust me."

I did not allow her to finish stumbling in darkness. The dam broke, and the water was not returning. "What do you expect? You have your cliques, and you discuss other people's business. You miss working for two weeks. I see you on Facebook in another country. The very day you get back, you pass all the indoor building rooms and come to my portable in the rain to see little ole me." Sam's unintentional giggle paused me. I continued, "Everyone knows you are after me, and it's a personal matter." Most principals seldom visited out of the building classrooms. The day Denise came to mine, heavy rain which normally deterred anyone's visitation, did not hinder her.

Denise, taken aback from my directness, responded with unsettled emotions, "I don't talk to anyone about the staff. If I need to, I discuss things with Sam and Paula."

Sam tried to support Denise at this point. "Darline, it's just the school environment. People talk with one another. Rumors happen all the time." I nodded in his direction and returned my attention to Denise. Sam's intentions were understandable. I did not believe Sam was aware of Denise's and Paula's behaviors towards me. More than likely, Sam tried to appear as a team.

"That's not true. And you even run around talking about Sam. Everyone knows how you and Paula treat him." I did not care Sam was sitting there. Unbeknownst to me, we wrapped up the meeting.

When I left the office, my portable suitemate, as we called ourselves, saw me as I walked down the hall. I walked faster when I heard her call my name. She knew about the meeting and followed quickly behind me. She often witnessed Denise frequently come to my portable. Our classrooms shared an inside door, and she observed the difference in treatment between us. She was a lifesaver many days with encouragement and understanding.

With curly blond hair, a very soft-spoken but spitfire personality, she attempted to engage me in conversation. She trotted behind the faster I walked. By the time she caught up, I was near my car. "Are you okay?"

I turned to speak but could not. I could not risk Denise and Paula, realizing they had gotten to me. Their arrogance would misunderstand my tears.

She asked again. This time I choked out a few words, "Not now. I'll call you."

I closed the door. She beckoned to let my window down. I was so angry with the veil removed from my eyes I was Paula's persistent target of racism. I wanted her just to leave me alone. But as God would have it, at my moment of confusion and intense hurt, a White woman looked at me to say, "I'm sorry. I want you to know I love you, and I'm here when you're ready to talk."

I nodded because one word would have opened the river of Jordan. In retrospect, it was a beautiful and spiritual moment. Whereas one White person was attempting to break everything in me, another was there to uplift, and I knew she meant what she said. There was never a moment I did not believe her. She was not the only White person who poured into me spiritually during my time under Paula's oppressive leadership. Those who were aware of the harassment texted encouragements and scriptures.

On my way home, I recollected emotionally. One of the Black teachers called wanting to follow up. I began to tell her the conversation. I arrived in front of my house and continued. I rambled emotionally, spitting every word with frustration. When I got to the details of telling Denise I did not like her or Paula, those words' weight resonated in me from my co-worker's response.

"Wait! Wait! McElroy! Go back. Stop! Pause! Go back! Did you just say you told her you didn't like her or Paula?"

"Yes, I did, and I don't. I'm sick of them!"

She laughed uncontrollably. Her laughter ignited mine for a moment until she asked, "What did your husband say?"

I paused. The words became heavier. Sure, my husband knew of the frequent observations and unprofessional write-ups. He assisted in writing rebuttals to their false claims. However, I had just made it home and did not speak to anyone until she called. He did not know the exchange in the recent meeting; he often advised me to stay calm and present facts, not emotions. In between my pauses and responses, she vehemently laughed that my anger relented, and I could not believe it either. However, I was okay with the responsibility for my words. It was time.

"McElroy, I cannot believe you told her you didn't like them! You said what everyone wants to say to their bosses but don't have the courage." She released a burst exuberant laughter. Hearing how she attempted to regain control, I chuckled with her. Several weeks after our conversation, she went in and out of the few Black teachers' rooms who knew about the incident, stood in the doorway, and repeated, "I don't like you!" Her comical expressions made the environment more palatable.

Released from most of the tension, I now had to share with my husband, a Pastor, and an educator his wife told her bosses t she did not like them or trust them. Being church leaders was a new role for us. There is a delicate balance of being true to self and respecting the responsibilities which come with leadership. My husband was aware of my frankness, but even in this, it was a stretch for me.

Leaving the call with my co-worker in full laughing throttle, I went into the house. As fate would have it, he was home earlier than usual from work.

Chapter 5

Honey, I'm Home

The older you become, and the longer you have been married, the less you desire to argue. Arguing takes days to recover. You realize the energy spent is not worth the fight, especially over other people's foolishness. Stress often induces intense discussions. Some things do not need discussion in a marriage is another lesson you eventually learn. However, this incident did not fall into the "no discussion needed" category. It was not the same as another Amazon Prime box arriving the same day as five others without it being a holiday.

God was working with my desire, my teenage prayer, to help me control my words. I once believed whatever I thought or felt, I had a right to voice. As a preteen, my mother regularly discussed the importance of words and tone. With five siblings, I had enough practice of saying the wrong things. The more my mom talked with me, the more I desired to change. I could see growth with age and experiences, but it was prolonged growth. I prided myself with speaking the truth but learned truth spoken harshly defeats its purpose.

My siblings and I were also encouraged to pray until a change occurred. Even if you are doing wrong, pray. The aftermath of saying things in frustration or anger weighed heavily. Therefore, I often prayed, asking God to change my speech intensity.

Because I did not see the change I wanted quickly, I criticize myself for being straightforward. I hated the passion and compassion I had when witnessing anyone not treated fairly. I knew in some situations speaking up was the right thing. Those who benefited thanked me for saying what they could not. However, I struggled between not wanting to speak up and the passion for equality.

To avoid harshness, I developed a coping skill of silence. I needed to process my feelings to understand what I felt and why. The problem with this strategy was my silence was to an extreme. My silence could last for days leaving others to believe I was angry, which was not always accurate. But the alternative was to say hurtful things.

It was in my marriage that my coping skill of silence created much friction. My husband's communication style of immediacy clashed with mine. In many intense discussions, he wanted issues resolved at the moment they occurred. I knew what lay ahead if I spoke before processing my feelings. Having the opposite communication styles was not pleasant. It landed us into marriage counseling, which planted the necessary seeds to grow better as partners. Through counseling, my husband and I managed our different communication styles.

I attempted the skills I learned with my administrators. I did not speak up about many things because of my efforts to respectfully consider their concerns. Hence, I owned the responsibility for their behaviors initially. It was now time to exercise the blessings of my voice, courage, and passion. Truth does not change because we are silent. Silence is usually not optional at a workplace, especially when the leaders' goal is to agitate to the point of emotional exhaustion.

My insecurities made a pathway for God to pour His word into me as I searched for Him in scriptures and prayer. I understood I represented Him and how He created me was without mistakes. I practiced honoring Him by loving all of me with respect to His boundaries. Everything about me was for His glory and use. Backing down and running away was not an option. To continue to allow oppression was unacceptable even if I was the only target.

I went over to the dinner table where my husband sat eating. I replayed the meeting details. He listened as he ate. When I got to the part of telling Denise I did not like them, he looked up. Calmly he inquired, "Do you think God told you to say that?" He turned back to his plate.

The conversation was about to get awkward. I focused on how to express my thoughts effectively. My usual hit straight needed a little curve flow. What I was about to say was not going to fare well in his mind. His perspective as an administrator usually came from that experience. However, the positive, in this case, was he had also experienced similar personal attacks.

After considering my prayers and intentions, I stood on my beliefs. Denise and Paula harassed me mercilessly. In the four years crippled with degrading, numerous meetings, and surveillance abuse by the assistant principals, Paula came to my classroom once at my request. I needed assistance with a student who refused to leave the room for lunch.

I did not have a hidden agenda for the meeting. This time, I intended to say nothing, document the meeting, and plan to leave the school for the next school year. I had no intention of trying to harm anyone with my words. In the past, I premeditated every word to counteract disagreements. I was not disrespectful to Denise, but I was very frank. I knew my husband's unannounced concern was probably this girl is about to get fired. And with four children on our tab and other expenses, we needed the income.

After contemplating my motives, I responded, "Yes, I think God led me to these words." I avoided quoting the Bible, though many scriptures came to mind for defense. Using scripture to defend yourself in a debate usually removes the context of that scripture. Without context, scriptures lose their intended purposes. It is a struggle to avoid, but necessary to practice.

He turned back to me, with an intensely confused expression I almost laughed. "Really? Do you think God would tell someone to tell another person they don't like them?"

He was about to discover if he did not already know, the fullness of whom he had married. "I actually do. I had no plans to tell them those things as I would have in the past. I was calm. Something came over me, and I honestly have no regrets."

He revealed his genuine concern. "You were insubordinate. You could lose your job."

"What? I have done my job and continue to do my job. Am I insubordinate to tell folks to stop mistreating me? Telling someone you don't like them is not insubordinate." I calmed down as I knew he had every reason for concern. We had a mortgage, car payments, bills, debt, and four children. I did not want this to be about us. It was not about our relationship, but about others who did not value another human being.

As we paused in our conversation, I reflected on the stress from the leadership's behaviors and how my countenance changed each day at work. Most Black students, considered "difficult" to manage, landed in my class at mid-year. My indoor classroom, replaced with an outdoor portable room, went to a White teacher. The day I moved into the portable, costumes and equipment covered almost every square inch. While others set up their classrooms with the coveted time we had, I had to wait until the room became available. A co-worker cleaned and decorated the room as I was giving in to the pressure.

The consistent surveillance counted more times than my department co-workers collectively. The constant push to label me as the stereotypical angry Black woman overwhelmed me. The blatant mistreatment was evident to those in my department or close to my classroom.

Although my co-workers frequently encouraged me, I bent under the load while responding to students' educational and social needs and career demands. Some days I just wanted to spit and walk out. My husband and I would make it work at home. I could substitute. We had learned how to live broke. I knew I could have quit earlier, but I desired the discipline of persevering in troubled times. Leaving was my go-to when stressed. Without perseverance, we cannot achieve any goal. I needed to learn how to stand under pressure.

I understood what happened in the office. It may have been unconventional, but this time my heart was in the right place when I approached the situation. No harm. Just take notes. Have a plan of action to leave at the end of the year. I had stayed long enough. I accepted the spiritual improvement, and this was as far as I could go. It was good enough for me.

I returned to the conversation. "Four years, they have tried to make me miserable, and they continued each year with more foolishness because they couldn't force me to leave. You know all the things they have done. If they dare to bully, I dare to have the courage to stand up. I am tired of it. In the Bible, does it tell God's people always to be silent in the face of evil? In the Bible, does it tell God's people we are doormats to be walked on constantly?"

After recapping the oppressive actions at Paula's hands, he consoled, "If after four years of dealing with all that, they're lucky, that's all you said."

His words sent me to cloud ninety-nine. "You are very right! They got off easy." I appreciated his support and calmness in dire situations. I did not need a companion with the same personality. The balance God gave between us helped and was necessary.

My family members became concerned, as well. My mom discussed with one of my sisters, a former educator, how my sister might help with a resolution. As with most parents, we do not want our children to experience difficulties. Mom did not realize this sister laughed as much as my co-worker. I encouraged my youngest sister to calm down, believing I would be okay. As an educator, she was familiar with the environment, fortunately, not the same experiences. My eldest and `more emotionally reserved sister, a nurse, questioned whether my hormones were unbalanced and if I needed medication. My hormones did not need balancing, the scales of justice did. I appreciated their compassion, even the laughter, but it was an experience I would not wish on my enemies, not even Paula.

It was time to depart. The relationship with the leadership was irreconcilable. The rumors about Paula were factual. Once she disliked you, there was no chance of changing her opinion. God decided it was time to transition, but He had more work than I realized before my departure. My response to Denise and Paula's harassment opened the door for the battle to come. Paula, replacing the arrows, launched every missile she could find.

"Let perseverance finish its work so that you may be mature and complete, not lacking anything." James 1:3 (NIV)

Chapter 6

98% Success Rate

It appears Genesis 5:24 (NKJV) acknowledges very little about the prophet, Enoch. The scripture simply states, "Enoch walked with God, and then he was no more because God had taken him away." There are short mentions in Jude and Hebrews as Paul's heroes of faith. which is an indicator of Enoch's relationship with God. Though little is mention of Enoch in the Bible, once you begin to walk with God in obedience and purpose, you realize to "walk with God" composes an entire book and lifetime. Most importantly, it requires faith.

As a babe in Christ, you may believe walking with God is a cakewalk, fun with a prize. Walking with God is beyond church attendance or your favorite hymn or praise and worship song. Discouragement on the journey causes many to turn away if we do not understand walking with God is exceptionally challenging. To be used by God is rewarding, for it is His design for our lives. However, the walk requires an unyielding faith in unfavorable circumstances to fulfill our spiritual stewardship. It is in the walk with God we discover our purposes in each life's seasons.

Many are perplexed and search for God's calling. The calling is not a mystery, as many believe. Dr. Diane Langberg puts it this way, "There is great hope in knowing God is not calling us to be bigger, better, or extraordinary. He wants to take the small, hidden, little, and seemingly unimportant things in our lives and inject them with eternal glory. We can rest in our commonness, our ordinariness, and our smallness."

Our calling is to do God's will in our homes, workplaces, churches, and everywhere we are sent or allowed to be. His will is the connecting thread that runs through every facet of our lives. We can confuse and miss the calling by searching for what we want to do based on what we like. We can also reduce the calling's effectiveness by focusing on other peoples' influence. Walking with God will not always fit into societal expectations. We can sometimes consider those who take a stand as unpatriotic or not operating in love.

Consider a few known for faith in Hebrews chapter eleven. How much effort, time, and the right attitude did it take for Abel to offer a more excellent sacrifice? Was it not faithful of Cain to bring what he had? Why couldn't Cain use the scriptural concept of "just come as you are?" Why did God care so much about the attitude of giving that He accepted Abel's offering but rejected Cain's? Why is Abel even listed as faithful just for giving?

Did Abraham leap for joy at having to leave for a foreign country without a definite residence? Did Abraham not love his nuclear family? Where were his upbringing and family's loyalty? Abraham trusted God, which went against his traditional upbringing.

Then there is Sarah, Abraham's wife. Do you know of any ninety-year-old women willing and enthusiastic to give birth to her first child? She tried to help God with the process, indicating her belief in God's promise. Although she believed God, Sarah did not trust His method. As usual, when we do not wait on God or do things according to His plans, the results hurt us. Sarah learned a valuable lesson about God's timing but is known for her faith.

Maintaining faith requires selflessness. How many people would choose affliction over wealth as Moses? Moses left

Pharaoh's luxuries, influence, and reputation connected with the rich and the famous.

Rahab, a prostitute, forsook her own country and people for the Israelite spies. The fact the writer of Hebrews listed a woman and a prostitute as faithful stands for itself. Examine Colin Kaepernick's consequences for kneeling during the national anthem to get an indication of Rahab's risk.

With all odds against them, our spiritual ancestors maintained uncompromising faith. They gave up expectations and personal desires to walk with God. They also placed their comforts aside, with some jeopardizing their and family lives.

We must not confuse purpose with career paths or hobbies. Faith and purpose often do not come in pretty or desired packages. We may not like what or where God allows, but it is not an indicator of misplacement or something gone wrong. God knows where you are going or what career you will choose. We are creative beings from the Creator. Therefore, there are career options. The question is, how will we allow Him to operate through us in our chosen careers?

God scatters His seeds in us. God's seeds are proficient. We determine whether the ground is productive, shallow, or rocky. And as with any quality ground, cultivation is required through prayer, studying, and applying God's word within our daily lives. The combination of prayer and application of God's word produces fruit. The fruit produced from Christ in us is the balm needed for healing the land; thus, bringing Heaven to earth.

I wanted God to trust His seed in me. Our behavior must indicate we are appreciative as redeemed Christians. I also understood it was imperative not to allow the need for acceptance to pull me into emotional abuse. We cannot allow the appearance of being a Christian override setting boundaries. Sure enough, we will have to endure one another's burdens and weaknesses;

however, this does not mean we become someone's emotional punching bag.

Jesus commanded us to love our neighbors as we love ourselves. To know how to love others, we must learn to love ourselves properly. Setting personal boundaries allows us to love ourselves and others better. If we set boundaries, then we know how to respect boundaries. Without understanding the totality of love, we grow spiritually imbalanced and not as useful to God.

Perhaps love would have been better shown had I said I do not like your treatment of me and gave examples instead of saying I do not like you. However, I did not have regrets even when things later got very rough. Though my truth may have been raw to the ears, my reality came from a rapidly degrading environment. A leader who sought to steal the light from within me, kill the strength given to me and destroy the little girl who God had built up. In this process of development, I learned to extend grace to myself.

Of course, you probably should not tell your supervisors you do not like or trust them when their leadership skills are inadequate and not expect repercussions. Some days I truly felt sorry for Denise, whom Paula influenced to execute what she did not dare to do. Other days, I did not understand how the fear of losing a job outweighed the respect of God's judgment. Even if it was friendship, authentic friendship should promote self-respect and not allow yourself to be used to mistreat another person. Perhaps Paula's influence tapped into the assistants' dark desires or weakness of understanding authority swaddled in responsibility.

The day after meeting with Denise and Sam, I returned to work. It was against my husband's advice to stay home to rest emotionally. I did not realize how discouraged and hurt I was until I saw Paula. Of all the times I heard of people snapping, I finally understood. She dashed through her office door the moment she saw me coming in the front entrance. Hiding was her typical response to any confrontation, although she was the initiator and sustainer of conflicts.

About thirty minutes to an hour later, I received an email from Sam stating he would be my evaluator. I was no longer on A.L.F.T.A. (Appraised Less Frequently than Annually), which meant I would have an unplanned appraisal this school year. This plan was part of the state's appraisal system which allowed teachers with proficient evaluations not to have formal observations yearly. I emailed and asked why, but I knew Sam would not respond in an email. So, I called. "Sam, what's going on?"

"Darline, I know this is sucky. I'm sorry."

"I need a substitute. I'm going home." I hung up my classroom's phone and called other team members. They were shocked and began texting advice on getting attorneys and reporting the principal. One team member was so distraught she encouraged me to contact Johnnie Cochran, a civil rights attorney, not realizing he was deceased.

I prepared my substitute plans and gave my first-period students their assignment. Fortunately, my second period was my conference time, so I did not have to smile and pretend for students before a substitute could arrive. Sam covered my class quickly. Before leaving the school, I saw two of my co-workers in the hallway. They attempted to comfort me, noticing tears in my eyes. I told them I would figure out something. I just had to work it out.

Sobbing once I got in the car, I called my husband. He left work to meet me at home. My older daughter opened the door as she did not expect me home this early. It was unusual for her to see me in this condition. She was silent. With tears streaming down my face, I silently passed by her to go into my bedroom. I went to my knees in prayer, seeking guidance and comfort.

As part of my upbringing, it was time for action. I was taught you could cry, but only for a moment. My mother's words, "You've cried enough," resonated crying is necessary at times, but you better get up and move on. Counselors called this resilience. My mama called it, "I'm going to give you something to cry about if you don't stop." I now fully comprehended the lesson. Life does not stop for tears nor do people's behaviors. If I did not pull it together and get a plan, I would have reasons to cry.

My husband made it home and helped me to sort the facts from the emotions. Afterward, I gathered all my documents to call a teacher's association attorney, who brushed me off by telling me racism claims were almost impossible to prove. She suggested I leave the campus. Then the attorney attempted to find common ground by comparing our personalities as outspoken. Her attempts to comfort by saying she left the education field to become a lawyer wasted my time.

I waited for God's guidance. I returned after a couple of days and requested a pre-conference with Sam, as my teammates suggested. It did not take a genius to figure out Paula's plan during the pre-conference with Sam regarding the formal observation. In the meeting, he mentioned he previously put two teachers on a T.I.N.A. or Teacher in Need of Assistance plan, which I had never experienced in 18 years as an educator. It was a growth plan acronym for teachers who were considered less than proficient and needed professional growth. I received this as a warning letting me know Paula's intentions.

Several co-workers insistently encouraged me to contact the area director after Sam's pre-conference to protect myself. Perplexed, I needed to sort out my feelings. It was a difficult decision. It is hard to trust an establishment that appeared to hire minorities as needed to maintain quotas. Besides, Paula had connections I certainly did not. I had only been in the presence of the area director twice. She visited the campus earlier in the school year, asking the faculty and staff about the environment. It was merely a staring contest between her and the staff.

I could not sleep a few nights until I made the decision the I would report Paula. The calmness and rest that came after the decision affirmed it was God's direction. Difficult but His path. Contacting the area director's secretary, I told her I wanted to report bullying, harassment, and racism. She suggested telling the principal. Initially, she did not comprehend what I reported as it was protocol to address issues with the principal first. After explaining twice, she finally understood I needed to meet with the area director concerning the principal's behaviors.

A couple of weeks later, I met the area director, Paula's supervisor, in her car in one of the district's building parking lot. I told her all the school's concerns as well as mine. She listened and took notes. We even shared a laugh when she thought I said Paula separated all the Black people from Whites by placing them in portable buildings. I assured her she would have heard sooner if that had happened, and it was not that kind of party.

My husband was appalled an area director met in a car. He believed the director knew the situation as accurate before meeting me or the district was unprofessional in many ways. Desperation meets anywhere. She waited for me to arrive after work, and I took what was available. It became an immediate need to meet with Paula as she worked quickly to implement whatever she had in mind. The area director called a meeting with the three of us.

I made up my mind this would be my last year at the school. I previously wanted to wait until obtaining a counseling position. Seeing how Paula could never call me to a meeting without an audience or respond to any of my emails was a reliable confirmation it was indeed time to leave. She would continue attempting to destroy my career. I figured I had grown enough by not running away the first four years. I also believed that it was time, and God's purpose ran its course.

Although the school's climate plummeted under Paula's leadership, she would remain. The staff completed several climate surveys without seeing results. Some staff members eventually stopped completing the computer-generated surveys. It was a waste of time and hope for change.

Before the meeting, I asked other Black staff members to give me their concerns. I warned, "If I can't attach your name to the comment, don't get involved. I don't need any backtrackers." I compiled a list and had a couple of teachers to review. It did not take long to compile a list as the campus significantly suffered under this principal's leadership. From the cafeteria workers, teachers, and my concerns, I prepared to present the information during the meeting.

Prior to the scheduled meeting with Paula and the area director, Sam completed my evaluation, focusing on classroom management and instruction. I was proficient in those areas. We discussed the review, but it had no value to me. I knew my work ethics were acceptable in doing my job well on any assignment I took professionally and personally. It was a common motto of my upbringing, "If you're going to do something, do it well or don't bother."

On the day of the meeting, I nervously grabbed my folder with the list of concerns and headed to Paula's office. Her appearance matched her character, frail. On her desk was a Dr. Pepper. The area director sat in a chair about three feet apart from me. At the start of the meeting, Paula's intentions and backstabbing plans came to the forefront. She mentioned the secondary human resource department director's name. I asked how the director got involved. Paula contacted the secondary human resource department director without my knowledge regarding evaluating me without proper procedures.

Sam's email only notified me he was my evaluator, and the observation window started the day I received the email. By policy, Paula should have had a meeting with me explaining the reasons for having to be evaluated. Of course, Paula was advised to do what was necessary. Principals' behaviors are challenging to track as they are assumed trustworthy and given autonomy on the campus. If the school's scores are high, it appears no one cares about the school's climate, which can be oppressive. If the principal has friends in the upper administration, every effort to report them is futile.

When given the time to express concerns, I addressed the overall climate for Black people first. I knew I could not return to the school, but I wanted those coming behind or remaining to have a better chance of equality and equity. Black teachers who were certified administrators lacked the opportunities to manage the office. However, White teachers, who did not have an administrative certification, periodically filled in for absent administrators. During my time at the school, there had not been a Black teacher of the year nor four years later.

Black students, compared to the white students committing the same behavior infractions, received harsher consequences. Black teachers most often taught regular classes instead of honors-level classes where the student population had a higher percentage of White students. Although the student population would benefit from a minority administrator, all administrators were White. They feared some of the Black parents or failed to establish connections with the lower socioeconomic students, mostly Hispanic and Black.

Once, I saw Paula escape from her office's back door when an upset parent screamed at Sam. The parent's claim her child's skin color determined the disciplinary consequences. I knew the student, so I called the mom to the school's foyer to intervene. Calming down, she explained why she was upset. After listening,

I encouraged her to take a different approach, but I understood her frustration. There were noticeable differences in disciplinary actions.

I further explained Paula excluded the cafeteria workers in staff activities, refusing to include them in the simplest things such as staff t-shirts. The cafeteria staff said that Paula did not speak and appeared to consider them as "the help." I pointed out Denise stated, "My child will never go to P.E. class," referencing the Black teacher who taught the class. Denise kept her word and placed her son in other courses where White teachers taught and were lenient with her child's disrespectful behaviors.

Paula leaned in so far over her desk, appearing pale and fragile, and insisted she was not aware. I did not know if she was ill or needed sleep. When Paula asked for names, I gave her two co-workers' names as she claimed to want the input from others to make improvements. In case she assumed I played her games of not telling, I came prepared.

The area director discussed an incident in which I was agitated with a student. In her investigation, students shared I was upset with a student who never brought in homework. I admitted to them this incident did happen. I then asked why one incident warranted constant surveillance and bullying tactics for almost five years.

I gave administrator names and incidences where I witnessed them screaming at students, which we often heard from behind their closed office doors. The area director responded since I was not in those meetings with the administrator and students during those times, I did not know whether the situations warranted those reactions.

I inwardly disagreed with their response; however, it was not my focus for the meeting. The truth was I did get upset and needed to take ownership of the incident. More so, I wanted my voice and others to be heard and valued. Paula gathered her strength as it appeared, she had her boss's support and remarked, "Darline, you just need to appear happier with the students. Homework is not that important to get upset."

It was time to call a spade a spade. "Are you indicating it's acceptable for White administrators and teachers to yell at the top of their voices, but my reactions indicate I'm an angry Black woman?" I guess Paula did not get the concept that inhabitants of the environment know the environment. And my daughter was a student in the honors classes where most of the teachers were White. The staff had just enough Black teachers dispersed throughout the school.

"I take offense to that," the area director stated, looking astonished at Paula.

Addressing the area director, I responded, "Don't. I'm just asking a question. I agree as professionals, we all should do our best not to become agitated and make children feel bad. However, if you are going to address it with me, certainly, the leaders should lead by example."

She accepted my response and encouraged me to continue. I told Paula I would no longer return as I was tired of staying two steps ahead of the games. She smiled in victory. I was not too fond of the feeling defeated, but it was apparent she would continue harassing me. The area director appeared to have her back during the meeting. The school's test scores were high ranking within the area as it was a magnet school. Good test scores meant everything was fine.

The area director, realizing Paula's satisfaction, quickly attempted to redirect the situation. "Mrs. McElroy, after my investigation, it appears you only had two concerned parents. That's a ninety-eight percent success rate." Glancing at Paula, the area director anticipated Paula would interject. The hinting glares did not matter to Paula; she basked and did not respond to my future departure. Paula finally hit the bullseye, and I did not have the energy to care. It was enough. I could no longer fight.

Later, I thanked the area director in an email, hoping for a response. Her personality in the car contradicted who she appeared to be in the meeting. I needed to know if I could be that far off in my judgment. To my surprise, she acknowledged my truth by thanking me for my honesty and courage to stand up to racism and noted new practices were needed. I could not believe she wrote this in an email, giving me documentation of Paula's behaviors. You only need new practices if old practices are ineffective. Filing the printed email in my closet one evening, I resolved I did my best, and it was time to move on.

Paula made a few momentary changes. She spoke to the two Black teachers whose names I gave. Paula allowed the two administrative certified Black teachers to manage the office a couple of times. The Black staff took notice and complimented my efforts. They believed I made a difference. I figured it would be short-lived, and it was. From Paula's response in the meeting, I knew she would not change if unchecked by her supervisor.

Within a few weeks, I received a promotion as an elementary school counselor. Sam came to my room, gave a high-five, and hugged me. The same White teacher who told me Paula and Denise's behaviors were racist was shocked when I told her I hugged Denise goodbye. Sullenly, she said, "I would have smacked them right across the face."

The idea of transferring from the school released such a burden I would have hugged Satan. I started the school counseling position within the district on April Fool's Day.

Chapter 7

Shattered, not Broken

Slowly Brock's behaviors unraveled like a spool of fallen yarn. It started with the day I asked the office secretary for chocolate. Along with the data clerk, she took us down the short hallway into Brock's office, where she said he kept candy for the staff meetings. The office secretary walked over to Brock's restroom, opened the door, and pointed to the small file cabinet that held the candy in the top drawer. She was stunned when the data clerk and I refused to eat the chocolate.

"What's wrong with it? "

"Who keeps candy in a nasty restroom?" I asked, looking at the data clerk who laughed in agreement.

"It's in a wrapper. It's not like it is on the floor. It's the same candy you have in the faculty meetings," the secretary responded.

I immediately declared, "And it's the last candy I will have in the faculty meetings."

Knowing the candy came from Brock's restroom gave me incredible restraint from eating or wanting chocolate during staff meetings. Perhaps because the secretary did not know about the CPS report, she found my response awkward.

My sentiments were confirmed by a few counselors who came to our school to assist with a crisis. Someone from the office put a basket of chocolate on my table for the guests. By the afternoon, a couple of the counselors wanted chocolate. I encouraged them not to eat it but did not want to tell them why. They continued questioning, initially thinking it was about the calories. When I revealed to them that Brock kept the candy in his restroom, in disgust, they quickly threw the candy back in the basket. One of the counselors placed the entire basket on the top of a tall file cabinet and washed her hands. I was often uncertain about my thoughts regarding Brock's behaviors. Their response to keeping candy in a restroom helped me not feel as though I overreacted.

Later, he put a giant teddy bear in his restroom he had forced a first-grade teacher to remove from her classroom. One morning on a group message, he texted he would be late, but the bear could handle things. One of the office staff members explained the text to me later. It was strange to her as well.

Brock also had the office staff to create and hang Ryan Gosling's hey girl memes with workplace quotes in the staff restrooms. It made a few teachers extremely uncomfortable, especially the seasoned teachers who Brock jokingly encouraged them to retire. Others reported a few unsettling behaviors, but I still heard nothing from the district's investigator. I did not know what else to do.

Some of the staff members decided to play "Elf on the Shelf" before the Christmas holiday break. Brock thought it was hilarious to put the elf inside the women's sanitary holder with the elf's eye peeping through the hole. When Mandy told me he put the elf in the sanitary holder, she indicated how repulsive his behavior appeared. She then shared with the office staff Brock placed the elf in the microwave after removing it from the restroom.

The burden of being in a building every day wondering what was going on, scared for children, and hearing other things about Brock was immense. I confided in a co-worker, Amerika, who mostly kept to herself. Amerika cried. She stated some people did not have the courage because they feared losing their jobs. We spoke of Mr. Rosario's report. She was uncertain of Mr. Rosario's validity regarding Brock's behaviors the previous year. Because I confided in her as well, she now believed Mr. Rosario's report.

I also shared with Amerika I believed Mandy had a significant part in Mr. Rosario's mistreatment. Mandy often remarked that Mr. Rosario did not value women nor respect her leadership as an assistant principal. Mandy and Mr. Rosario frequently had very cordial conversations during lunch, so I just believed it was a moment to moment thing with her.

The previous year before Mr. Rosario's transfer, Mandy pulled me into my office one day to ask about the conversation I was having with his two teammates. "Hey, so what are y'all talking about?"

Confused as to why anyone would ask about a conversation, they were not a part of, I responded, "What?"

She laughed before sharing, "Did they tell you Mr. Rosario's assignment will be first grade next year?"

Mr. Rosario was an opinionated Hispanic male who was very good with his fifth-grade students and parents. He appeared very stern and introverted. From our conversations, after a few times, it was easy to see Mr. Rosario cared about his students and their school performance.

Moving teachers to a different grade level, especially with such an age gap, was a principal's strategy to discourage them from returning. It was an effortless and sometimes retaliatory tactic that required no documentation or coaching. A teacher's removal, if done correctly, required documentation of coaching assistance on a growth plan.

"Does he want to be moved to first grade?" I asked.

Mandy stopped smiling as she realized it was not entertaining to me.

"Well, he said he wouldn't mind. It would give him a chance to see the expectations of students in the lower grades." She quickly left my office. I distanced my interactions from Brock and Mandy. There was no way Brock, in his first year, could have this amount of ill-will towards Mr. Rosario unless Mandy set the stage. I did not want to be associated with mistreating others. Later, Sally, laughed as she told me about Mr. Rosario's plight. She, often privy to staff concerns through Mandy, revealed information.

Before I left her office, Amerika hugged me and said she was proud of me. She cried again. I found myself comforting her instead of being consoled. I assured her I would be okay, and God is my source with the job only a resource. I left her office but returned when I passed by and saw her eyes were still red as though she had continued to cry after I left. I reminded her everything would go according to God's plan.

Later in the school year, Brock became passive-aggressive. During an office staff celebration, Brock rarely spoke of his family as he did this day. He blurted without prompting, "Yeah, my brothers are coming to town." When no one responded to the comment, he repeated, "Yeah, my brothers are coming this weekend, and they are both attorneys. Yep, both attorneys."

An office clerk finally asked, "Why don't you invite them to the school for us to meet them."

Shaking his head as though she asked him to eat dried dog food, he stated, "Oh no! I don't mix work and personal things." His attempt to intimidate was futile. It made me more aware of his insecurities, and I did not care by this point. I was mentally exhausted from the rumors about Brock, people confiding in me in how the administrators treated them and experiencing his, Mandy's, and Sally's behaviors. I did not care if every member of his family were attorneys. I would still stand on what I believed.

The morning Brock spoke loudly and heartily, as I entered my office, I realized Brock relaxed in his expectations of any consequences. And I realized no one was going to tell me anything about the incident with the child. Because I had not seen the videos, I fluctuated between thoughts of seeing things wrongly and knowing I saw correctly.

By the time December rolled around, I was more apt to go with the normal. I pulled Brock's name for the Christmas gift exchange. I decided to go along to get along when Mandy offered to exchange people for Secret Santa. By this time, I knew she had more in common with Brock, and only God knows what other fire she would add to the flames. With the previous school's bleak experiences ingrained, I was more conscious of my words and actions.

Other than Amerika, I told no one about the incident about the child. My silence gave away when Brock sent an email to come to his office one day in January. It concerned the child who Brock allowed to touch him inappropriately.

I went to his office as requested and stood at the entrance. Sitting at his round table near the doorway, he announced, "Effie's parents finally agreed to the testing for Effie. I have established a good relationship with the parents. Since the evaluation is sensitive to them, I will facilitate the meeting." Facilitating these types of meetings was one of my primary roles as a school counselor. Of course, being the principal, he could do as he pleased.

I tried to maintain my facial expression. "Oh, okay."

Brock requested, "So just get me the paperwork I need for the meeting."

"Will the diagnostician be in the meeting, too?" I questioned to calculate Brock's intentions. The diagnostician was not usually in this kind of meeting.

"No, just us, the parents, and the teacher."

Brock's deception burned within me as I returned to my office. When you are in a position where you cannot call out someone's deceit, but you see the dishonesty, it is demoralizing. Within an hour, that feeling turned into anger when Brock entered my office and asserted, "Effie's parents don't want you in the meeting, so I will just facilitate it."

I attempted to offset the shock I felt. He smiled as he twirled a pen in his mouth, enjoying my facial expression. "That's fine. Just one less thing I have to do." Later, I emailed the diagnostician to get the necessary paperwork for the meeting. Keeping up with Brock's games required constantly thinking ahead.

Mind games uproot your instincts. Brock lied for certainty. However, I wondered at times did the parents believed I called CPS in malice. I could not imagine any parent not understanding the goal to protect unless Brock convinced them. Consistent lies permeate your thoughts at times. You must always force yourself from the barrel of lies to know what the truth is.

Brock's cunning behaviors required steady alertness. Once, he encouraged me to go home early after an off-campus training, which required both our attendance. Thinking I followed his advice, he boasted to the office staff how he promptly returned to the campus after the training. When Brock saw me coming from my office, he was shocked. He questioned why I did not go home. I told him about the work I needed to complete, so I decided to return to the school. He encouraged me to finish and leave as soon as possible. I did not fall for Brock's plan to discredit my character. I walked away from him thinking, *my mama didn't raise a fool*.

Before the parents' meeting, I emailed Brock offering my office, which was the usual place. Since I planned to only be at work half of the day, it would be available. It was also a way to include the student's name for documenting Brock's interference with my responsibilities. He refused to use my office but conducted the meeting in a room near Effie's classroom.

The meeting was held without me, as Brock planned. But as God would have it, a therapist, who was a part of the meeting, walked out as I walked past the room to leave. Pulling me aside, angered and frustrated, he snapped about Brock, "I cannot believe what just happened in this meeting. Those parents ripped into the teacher, and Brock did not defend Ms. Gallegos! She was in tears as they blamed her for everything and called her very negative."

Ms. Gallegos nurtured all children. We were in constant contact initially regarding Effie's adjustment to routine and expectations. She attempted to make a connection with the family but only received abusive responses. For Brock to allow the parents to mistreat Ms. Gallegos again would discourage her efforts. "Where is Ms. Gallegos now?" I inquired.

"She left upset. And after all that, they still refused to sign the evaluation paperwork."

Speechless, I shook my head. However, I was glad Brock saw he was not as convincing to everyone as he thought. He was overconfident in his ability to get the parents to agree with evaluating the student. Now, these two staff members also gained insight into his character.

We went into Ms. Gallegos' room across the hall to see if she was there. She was not. As we stood in Ms. Gallegos' room, the therapist continued, "I cannot believe he would allow that!" I had not seen him this angry before. It must have gone badly. He continued expressing his frustration and disappointment in Brock. Before ending the conversation, he requested I not tell Brock about the conversation. He did not realize I would not have told Brock that a blazing fire was in the building.

The next morning, during a scheduled read-aloud for Ms. Gallegos' kindergarten class, Ms. Gallegos asked to speak to me as

I was leaving. I expected she desired to discuss the meeting, but more than I expected was shared.

Ms. Gallegos repeated the details of the meeting. I gave specifics behavioral strategies she used, and how she tried to communicate with the parents consistently. I explained I had not received any additional notice of Effie's behaviors, so I thought Effie had improved. Knowing Brock manipulated the meeting, I asked if she knew that I would not facilitate the conference.

She responded, "No. Why did he exclude you?"

At this point, I lost concern for protocols. I told her I had reported Brock to CPS. I did not care about the district anymore. If the leaders did not care about protecting children, I was as free in my speech as their negligence. If the videos proved Brock's innocence, someone should have informed me. I wanted her to know that it was not my decision to be absent. I could usually reason with parents while supporting the student's best interest and the teacher's efforts.

Moving closer to the door in the back of her room, she lowered her voice, "One day I called Brock because Effie was having a rough day. When she saw Brock coming, Effie pulled down her pants."

"What?"

"Yeah. Brock asked me if Effie had done that before. I told him no. She only pulled her shoes off at times."

Usually, when very young students exhibited behavioral problems, I was most likely called to assist the teacher. However, in the case with this child, Ms. Gallegos shared Brock repeatedly came when Effie had disciplinary problems. And there were times he took her alone. Deflated, I could do nothing more but listen. She connected the pieces of Brock's actions during the meeting and why he allowed the parents. I asked if he said anything to her after the meeting with the parents.

She replied, "No. Pointing to her desk, "When I came in this morning, there was a Dr. Pepper and chips on my desk. I am assuming he placed them there. Who else would have?" Being disgusted with him, she did not want it.

Hopelessly, she asked, "Well, what do I do when Effie has behavior problems, and can't control her? Who do I call for her?"

"I don't know. I will come if you call me. I've done all I can do."

Shortly after this conversation, I told a couple of the office staff who previously expressed concerns about Brock's behaviors. I wanted them to look out if they saw students alone in his office.

A few days later, one of the office staff members confided Brock had a student alone with a locked door. When the incident initially happened, she felt strange but did not know what to think or what to do. Unaware of the district's investigator unprofessionalism, I advised the office staff member to contact Janie Lang. She emailed over the weekend and reported the incident.

The following week, while I was at an off-campus staff development, I received a text from the office co-workers that Janie Lang was interviewing a few students. She also had the office secretary in the room. I was confused about why the office secretary joined the investigation. Just like my report, nothing became of these interviews either. Those who knew were at a loss and felt Brock was indispensable regardless of his behaviors. After receiving the district open records, I decided to alert the district's leadership of five leaders who decided student's well-being nor mine mattered.

Chapter 8

Pressed, not Crushed

Easter Sunday morning and two days after being ridiculed in my co-workers' presence, my preaching assignment was to preach one of Jesus' seven sayings on the cross, "It is Finished." I prayed to have a heart of forgiveness towards Brock, Mandy, and Sally and move forward. To stand in a pulpit angry with others is often easily detected. How could I preach without forgiveness?

Before we all walked into the sanctuary, I shared with my husband that my mind labored over Brock, Mandy, and Sally's previous actions. There was no way I could neglect the preaching responsibility, so I prayed. Interestingly, I was not angry, but I was very saddened. It is tiresome to experience consistent racism. The adage, "Do right and right will follow," sometimes releases darkness.

The sermonettes before mine were uplifting. I prepared as best as time allowed between work, home and family, and church responsibilities. With my husband as the Pastor, personal expectations demanded I focus on the task ahead within the seven minutes limit.

One of the ministers preached, "Forgive them, for they know not what they do." Before preaching, I repeated this scripture to help me focus. I needed to allow my spirit to rest in God, fighting what my mind desired, to be home. In the past, disturbing events stifled my desire to engage with life. I usually succumbed to the circumstances.

Sunday, in most instances, was a spiritual high. It was easy to live in the moment of forgiveness sitting in church, surrounded by fellow Christians' strength. Monday morning dawned on the struggle. Headed towards the main office, I saw Sally. Sheepishly, she asked, "How are you?" Like a lion's roar, out went Sunday, and in came Monday!

Having to sign a greeting card in the nurse's office, the nurse and I discussed the cake mockery again. Together, we agreed I could not prove what they did. So, I must go on. Besides, I had earlier questioned the custodian about the whereabouts of the cake. She saw the cake and wondered why I trashed it. I was willing to dig in trash mounds to find the cake if necessary. However, it was too late to recover.

Walking down the hallway to my office, I silently repeated, "Father, forgive them for they know not what they do." When Christians desire to grow in Christ, we often war between our flesh and the Spirit. My flesh wanted to invoke Samuel L. Jackson's cursing spirit with the three stooges. Though we may refrain from old habits, we never forget. Samuel L. Jackson's ability to curse was an art form so well-articulated it left nothing to be assumed. Desiring to be like Sam, I prayed, "Father, forgive them, for they know not what they do."

Leaving my office to handle teachers' requests for items, I walked to the kindergarten hall with a returned feeling of light-heartedness and blessings from Sunday service. The sun, beautiful with full rays, extended through the glass doors lighting the hallway. I prepared my heart for the day's goals and to be present for those who needed assistance. Be at peace.

Not even fifteen minutes later, as I delivered the requested materials to teachers, rumors of the cake with alcohol confronted me. Another co-worker experiencing the leadership's wrath was putting her students' uneaten breakfast in the communal trash can. Upon seeing me, she approached and stated she heard about the cake. Vehemently, she encouraged me to report them.

When experiencing hardship as she was, it is easy to want others to join in the battle. I allowed her to express her frustration without the temptation to react. I understood the pain and desire to push back. She was a passionate and outspoken Hispanic woman who was also Brock's and Mandy's target. This commonality made us closer. She believed I had enough evidence concerning the cake to do some good for minorities within the district.

I chuckled as she attempted to recruit me as leader of an unknown and unprepared army, "Come on, McElroy. Do it! Do it for all of the minorities."

It was very comical listening to her as she reminded me of my younger self. She had not known me long. If anything, I needed encouragement to remain calm and silent. I wanted to be in a different spiritual place. I had a spiritual obligation to exemplify Christ. Though I did encourage her to advocate for herself, I also caution her to do it with facts and not emotions.

She went back into the classroom. I walked away, understanding her passion, but I did not want to join where God was not leading. I truly wanted to let it go and forgive them as they knew not what they had done. How do you come from preaching the day before and then desire to retaliate? I did not mind standing up, but I wanted to make sure the battle was the Lord's and not mine.

I walked next door to give a testing calendar to another teacher. Grinning like a new contestant for the Price is Right, she stated, "I heard about your cake."

"What did you hear?" She did not denote the tone of my voice or facial expressions as her two teacher's assistants did. She was genuinely having a happy moment alone.

"Well, I asked for a slice, and someone told me it had alcohol in it and that I didn't want it."

"Who told you?"

"I have my sources," she proudly retorted.

"Is that right? Well, I'm going to make a formal report, and I will include your name as having knowledge of the alcohol in the cake." Our relationship was one of fondness, so I knew she did not understand or intended harm.

Jolted with a clear understanding of the difference between my reactions and hers, she became speechless. Within a couple of minutes from one teacher, I decided this was worth my time and energy. The reality of what happened hit with every step I took. From one teacher to the next, before I could get my day started, truth invaded.

Looking at her two expressionless assistants, she realized the magnitude of the conversation. "Wait, wait. You don't drink? I thought you were American. Don't all Americans drink?"

"I guess I'm not American." We stared at each other as she tried to understand.

Confused, she asked, "What are you?"

"I'm a person who doesn't drink alcohol."

She attempted to soften the conversation by trying to reason. "Maybe it was just a joke."

It was fascinating about fifteen minutes before this conversation, the school's nurse and I discussed an example of giving someone pork who did not eat pork. "If I gave you food knowingly with pork, allowed you to eat it, and then revealed it had pork in it, would it be a joke?"

After responding with no, she motioned me away from her two assistants outside of the room. She apologized for disregarding my feelings. I repeated her name would be in the report as knowing the cake had alcohol. I also explained to disregard someone's religious beliefs and health should never be a joke.

A few moments later, one of her teacher's assistants saw me in the hallway and shared she was the person who gave the information. After the birthday celebration, the assistant saw Sally in the hall, laughing about the cake. Because of Sally's demeanor during the conversation, the teacher's assistant advised the teacher not to get a slice of cake. I emailed the district's investigator shortly after the assistant informed me.

Brock's behavior continued after school, confirming I needed to take a stand. The school day ended with a colleague's baby shower in the school's library. It did not matter to Brock that I did not come near the serving table. He raised his voice to get my attention when he saw me. As I walked to a table, Brock, serving the refreshments, asked if I wanted the punch. I declined.

He stopped serving and walked to my table. Brock loudly called out to Mandy, seated with Sally at another table. Extending his hand with the cup in the air, he quipped, "Hey Mandy, it's Tiramisu punch," and sat next to me.

Mandy snickered, "Stop it."

He was a new level of foolishness. Dumbfounded by his arrogance to sit by me and taunt, I asked, "What did you just say?"

Without a flinch or stutter, he brazenly stated, "I said it's a Tiramisu punch."

I did not respond. No one in the room would have understood had I reacted the way I desired. I texted the three ladies in the office since they witnessed the cake incident. They were in disbelief.

Not wanting to make a scene, I sat there, and flashbacks of the school year's beginning entered my mind. Brock and Mandy showed sobering video clips during staff development. One was the "Office Space Cubicle and Workplace Management" scene and the other YouTube clip on "Millennials in the Workplace Training." Most of the staff just sat and stared with a couple of awkward giggles. I asked a couple of people later the possible connection or reasons for the videos, and they were just as confused.

Sitting next to Brock reminded me of those videos and how I believed then it was a foreshadow of things to come. Those things were now my present. I sat there knowing, as he and Mandy alone with Sally lived their best life at my expense. If I had not had positive relationships with White people, hatred might have taken hold of my heart. And I understood their actions were a lack of Christ in their lives.

During the baby shower, Brock's taunting strengthened my resolve to make sure he and Mandy's behaviors stopped. As he brimmed in wickedness, I settled my heart, knowing soon he and his two accomplices' smiles would change. I left the baby shower sooner than I wanted. I could not continue sitting beside Brock.

I left the school and called a voice of reason. I hoped my dear and trusted friend had the time to answer my call. Feeling like a fool on a massive display, I questioned, "Am I that greedy that I didn't stop eating the cake as soon as my throat started to burn?" I chuckled insincerely. The emotional highs and lows pendulum was never-ending.

With conviction, she encouraged, "You needed to eat the entire slice. God knew you would not be offended enough to do anything about it." She stressed and slowly emphasized her beliefs again, "You needed to eat the entire slice." I acknowledged her passion but was not entirely in agreement. I just went with the ebb and flow of the conversation, trying to make sense of it.

As a former co-worker of the middle school where Paula was the principal, she provided support many days when I confided in her about Paula's and the assistants' harassment. After the promotion, I received phone calls and text messages asking for advice and how to deal with the constant racism and harassment. It left me feeling like a failure. I possessed the email for the area director that may have been able to have the principal removed. She encouraged me when I felt I had not done enough at the previous school. My friend was adamant others needed to take up the mantle, and I had done what God required.

It was one of my barren days. I understood disliking someone. I understood having a professional relationship, but not personal with someone you hated. I understood severing a relationship and moving on. But this was so beyond my comprehension I struggled to make sense of it every day since the incident. How can adults behave so immaturely and carelessly, especially in the workplace? What did God want from this?

Now it was time to fight the same battle with the same sword, but new energy. I knew without a doubt God sent me to the school. Though a sheep surrounded by wolves in power, I was a sheep who had a Shepherd. I had no reason to fear for their presence was only a shadow. By faith, I trusted Jesus would guide me in the path of righteousness for His namesake. In times of hurt, He would anoint me for healing and authority. I did not expect it to be easy, but I did not expect it to be as burdensome.

Chapter 9

Perplexed, not Despaired

One of the many demeaning strategies bullies engage is to make the target the brunt of their jokes in others' presence. Intentional, but it is an easy way to escape accountability if caught. Reporting the so-called joking makes the target look insecure and fragile. Brock decided I would be his target again the day after his bullying during the baby shower.

I facilitated a Student Support Team meeting which included a parent, Brock, and two other staff members. During the meeting, Brock attempted to hide behind coarse joking by implicating I was challenging to work with as a colleague. As I completed paperwork for the parent at my computer, I heard awkward giggling from the meeting participants' table. The giggling prompted me to turn around. Brock's hand was extended and pointed towards me. He quickly dropped his hand, and this was my breaking point.

His behavior now extended from a small office gathering to the entire staff, and now in front of a parent. Brock later admitted his actions to the district's investigator, but his admittance did not matter. Swirling entirely around in my chair, I leaned over towards the seemingly uncomfortable parent sitting between us. Glaring at Brock with direct eye contact, I responded, "Yes, mom, he's right! Some people are very difficult to work with!"

Brock's skin flushed red, and he murmured, "Well, I guess I better stop."

I agreed, "I guess you better shut up." We passed the paperwork around the table for signatures. I gathered the papers to make copies for the parent. Fuming, I went down the hallway into the main office to use the printer.

The office manager, whose desk was adjacent to the copier, quickly turned around when she saw me. "Hey, did you report the cake?"

With intensity, I responded, "I sure did!" I had not told the front office staff about reporting the cake to the district's investigator. I wanted a truthful and in the moment perspective, even if in disagreement.

The office manager informed, "Janie Lang, the human resource department's investigator just walked in. She went to the kinder hall."

Steaming over to the office aide, who assisted visitors with signing in, I firmly stated, "Good, before she leaves, tell her I sent another email about Brock. I'm sick of him, and I will not tolerate this anymore!" The office aide stammered, asking for clarity. It was the first time in two years she had seen me in this mode. She wanted to know how to tell the district's investigator my request.

I returned to my office, professionally and calmly, gave the parent her copies within a manila folder. After everyone left, I put on gospel music for about an hour, seeking God's guidance and comfort. Parents, visiting for lunch, peered through my window because of the music's volume. I did not care. The volume's intensity drowned my racing thoughts, so it was best for us all. I filed paperwork and cleaned and organized my office to aid the calming process.

I decided to reach for any help possible. The interim counseling director, Jennifer Starks, assisted after the counseling department director's demotion. She appeared to have an authentic concern for the department and the counselors. I decided to take a chance. I emailed the counseling department's interim supervisor, briefly explaining the situation and requesting assistance.

Shortly after sending the email, I went to the main office. To my surprise, the interim counseling director, Jennifer Starks, and Olivia Martin, one of the counseling department coordinators, were signing in. Within seconds, Janie Lang came to sign out. Jennifer asked Janie Lang to join us in a meeting if she had the time. Janie agreed. We walked to my office, and all sat at the circular table. I described the recent events about the cake, the baby shower's comments, and the parent meeting that prompted my email to Jennifer Starks.

Janie paused my explanation and addressed the interim director, "Darline and Brock have a history."

Making eye contact with me, Jennifer Starks looked for an explanation. I explained the CPS report. After I gave the background information, Janie stood up. She gave a demonstration of what the video recording indicated. Pushing both arms away from her body, she stated, "What Brock didn't do was push the child away."

This moment was the first and only time Janie Lang said anything verbally or written regarding the CPS report I filed on August 23 at the beginning of the school year. It was now April 24. Almost an entire school year Brock remained on campus.

After many agonizing days and nights wondering if I saw the wrong thing, I finally received my answer. What I witnessed was the truth. Not once did Janie ever contradict what I reported or what I wrote in my written report. Making matters worse, Janie excused Brock's behavior by reducing his actions to a mistake of not pushing the child away. A mistake even children knew better not to allow. If a student let the same actions Brock allowed with another student, protocols mandated a call to the parents, CPS, and corrective actions of possible suspension or alternative school.

I sat quieted by amazement that not one person from the district gave any report. A man sat as an elementary school leader on the campus with over five hundred vulnerable children, quoting, "Do what's best for children." However, this so-called leader did not have enough emotional intelligence or morals to do what he preached for children or adults. And in front of me, demonstrating what was evident in the video, was the lady responsible for his presence. More so, she was the culprit to children's safety by minimizing the incident, the second similar reported. Janie sat down.

I resumed telling them about the cake and the email Brock sent after the incident. I went to my computer, fumbling to locate the email. Olivia suggested that I put his name in the search bar. I printed and handed it to Jennifer Starks.

After reading to herself, Jennifer read the subject line aloud, "Can you get drunk off tiramisu! Why would anyone send this?" She then looked confusingly at the district's investigator. "This is harassment! What are you all going to do about him?"

Stillness permeated the room as we all looked at Janie Lang, who blankly stared at Jennifer.

Jennifer interrupted the silence, "Darline, I cannot tell them what to do with Brock. It is out of my range of responsibilities. I suggest you transfer. I have never seen anyone this determined to hurt someone."

I confided, "I have made it my personal goal to stop running from problems." It was my spiritual goal as well, but I did not announce it. God and I had an agreement; I could not leave until He directed me.

Olivia rallied, "Yeah! It's like the bully wins!".

Janie Lang's response indicated she felt pressured to comment. It was equivalent to watching an amateur actor versus Denzel Washington for a leading role. Slamming close her brown leather-like notepad portfolio and with a raised voice, she snapped, "I have told him about watching his words. I am tired of him! I am going now to talk very sternly to him. Janie stormed out of the office.

Ignoring Janie's foolishness, I repeated my stance to Jennifer. "Why should I leave? I am not the one who has done wrong. I have had similar experiences at my previous school. I had planned to leave before being promoted. Asking me to leave while the ones who did the wrong stay, isn't right."

With wisdom and gentleness, Jennifer suggested, "Darline, this is not about running away. It is about your safety."

Jennifer had a valid point. She had several years of experience from another large district. It was clear I was unsafe here. Sure, I had my office with a personal refrigerator, but the office staff and Sally had a master key. For this reason, I started bringing pre-packaged, store-bought, and sealed Hillshire lunches and checking to ensure they remained sealed. I stopped bringing leftovers for fear they would put something in my food.

Thankfully, my husband gave me a fifty-dollar Starbucks gift card as a Christmas gift. It purchased several lunches and gave me the respite during the day that was much needed, although, it was only twenty minutes. I was uncomfortable in my own space, not knowing what Brock, Mandy, or Sally planned. I needed to give thought and prayer to her guidance.

Jennifer explained the transfer process. By this time, Janie returned and informed she reprimanded Brock again. She had also spoken with Mandy. As Janie continued discussing her conversation with Mandy, I recognized Janie's biases. "Mandy said she had no idea alcohol was in the cake." Contorting her face to make her next statement meaningful, Janie followed up with, "She was very remorseful."

"Remorseful!" I retorted. An unspiritual vision occurred. *I leaped across the table and shook Janie to bring some sense in her mind.*" She didn't say one word to me as I complained of the burning sensation. If someone brings a dish, a cake, and another person complains of burning, the common sense and decent thing to do is ask what is going on with the food item you bought. You don't smile and walk out!"

Janie rebutted, "Mandy said she was afraid to say anything because then she would appear guilty." Mandy had the district's investigator full support. No one said anything but stared at Janie. She broke the silence. "But I will call the company to see what the ingredients were in the cake."

Jennifer repeated the transfer offer and encouraged me to talk with my husband about it. I understood she knew my husband but did not divulge that information. However, I did not understand what Jennifer expected my husband to do. Upon leaving, Olivia leaned over and hugged me tightly, encouraging me to hang in there.

With only Janie and I remaining in my office, standing at my door to leave, she asked, "Darline, do you really want to stay at this school?"

"Yes, I really do." Janie finally appeared concerned, but it was just the devil handing the fruit to eat.

"I will talk with the upper admin today."

Before returning the student's records in the main office, I threw away the triangular folded paper from Brock that read, "Do what's best for children." In the main office and looking as though he saw a ghost, Brock leaned against the file cabinet, pretending to be on his laptop. Once again, I reserved all my boxing maneuvers for the punching bag at home. I could not prove harassment from jail. Brock waited for the folder of the student discussed in the meeting during our unfriendly discourse. Realizing his patterns, Brock probably called the parent ahead of Janie Lang.

I called a counselor friend on my way home to discuss the day's events. The transfer period was over, so she knew something happened. She wondered the reason for the email the interim counseling director sent. Talking with her helped me to process. I could not allow people to give me an alcohol loaded cake, laugh as my throat and chest burned, tease me through email, and humiliate the following week. For the remainder of the year, Brock and his buddies' degrading behaviors would increase if I did not push back.

We were on the phone when I arrived home. I decided to email all those who had previously discussed the events the afternoon in my office. When I shared my plans to attach the email from a former White area director regarding racism, my friend advised me to take some time to think. I knew reason did not elude me, and calm was not a factor. To everything, there is a season, and it was not the time to run. It was time to take a righteous stance. Besides, if I agreed to transfer, I would have been forced to remain on campus with Brock and Mandy until the end of the school year. Transferring was not a solution, even at a minimum.

As soon as I opened the work account, I saw Janie's email stating she had called the bakery. According to Janie's investigation, the cake had no alcohol, but espresso coffee was in the cake. It confirmed my beliefs about Janie's biases during the meeting. I knew she lied about the bakery's statement.

Interestingly, earlier in the day, Sally came into my office with the same espresso coffee story. To convince me she was not laughing that my throat and chest burned, Sally said the Tiramisu cake was her first experience. Sally insisted she thought the strange taste was espresso coffee. She called the cake special during lunch the day we had the cake because it had come from an expensive bakery. With tears in her eyes, Sally pleaded with me to forgive her.

There was no more doubt regarding the three stooges. Finding a balance between reality and trauma is difficult, especially when inflicted emotional abuse is skilled with deception. We must learn it is necessary to judge rightly so that we do not subject ourselves to damaging abuse, which often distorts perception. I fully accepted Sally, Brock, and Mandy's behaviors were their real characters and my past experiences were not a factor.

However, I had a choice to make with Sally. How was I going to behave as a fellow Christian was the question in my heart? She came to my office to apologize. I knew the probability of her lying was high. Sally's character came to full light, and my character was on the line. The commitment to my faith was more important than my feelings towards Sally. The guidelines are different by Christian standards when a sister in Christ attempts to make things right. "If a brother or sister sins, go and point out their fault, just between the two of you. If they listen, you have won them over" (Matt. 18:15 NIV).

I did not believe Sally was sincere. Her fake tears irritated my soul. For this reason, I did not want to take a Biblical approach. However, I understood one plants the seed and the other waters, but only God makes things grow. It was an opportunity to plant, doing the work of God and not of myself. It was also an opportunity to put in practice my prayer of speaking appropriately in frustration.

Going against verbally attacking her with the Holy Spirit's help, I approached the conversation. "I don't believe you are honest. You profess Christ often and attend church religiously. You are supposed to be my sister in Christ."

With more tears flowing, she pleaded, "I know. I am your sister in Christ! I consider you a friend. I would never do anything to harm you."

Sally, calling herself a friend, revealed the depths of her manipulation. "I don't believe you know I am one of the people you talk poorly about, but I don't treat you any differently." Learning most people will have a conversation about you no longer bothered me. What a person said determined the type of interaction I would have with them. She was not in my inner circle, so it was unnecessary to hold her to a friendship standard.

Sally stopped crying. "Darline, I'm very honest. If I had something to say about you, I would tell you."

I again felt as though someone placed me in a beginning acting class, and I wished for the ability to projectile vomit. I ended the conversation by telling Sally if she were sorry, I would have no choice as a Christian but to forgive. If she were not genuine, God would deal with her.

The same day Sally came into my office, Mandy went to the nurse who also ate the cake. Crying to the nurse, Mandy stated how hurt she was people would consider her a monster. The nurse asked Mandy why she never came to speak with me, and her answer was the same she gave to Janie Lang of not wanting to appear guilty. The nurse suggested Mandy discuss the situation with me. Mandy claimed she was afraid. Typical.

I did not tell the nurse about my hurt feelings from how she could believe Mandy after sharing the experience with me and knowing Mandy's daily behaviors. I remembered the nurse reported the truth to the district investigator. She could have hidden the facts about the cake. As she gave me the advice to let go and believe Mandy was unaware, I knew she had good intentions.

It was understandable she believed Mandy's account of not knowing there was alcohol in the cake. Often those who have a compassionate heart trust the tears of manipulation. However, I intended to stand firm on the truth, and not the nurse's emotions.

These incidents reaffirmed my commitment to send the email. I returned an email to Janie, asking how to obtain videos from the surveillance cameras. Janie responded that she forgot about viewing the videos until I mentioned it. I had to request the videos from the district's legal team.

I located the 2016 letter regarding the meeting with Paula and the former area director. I overlooked part of the former area director's response for some unknown reason. Like a flashing green light was the second line, "*I wished we could've ended better, but it is what it is.*" There were no words to describe this statement as I had killed the term foolishness over the past weeks. Later, I understood the magnitude of "it is what it is" as the events would begin to play out. However, "it is what is" was not going to be my reality.

I emailed Jennifer Starks, Olivia Martin, and Janie Lang, attaching the 2016 email response. *Thank you all for your support today. I have decided that I do not want to leave the campus. I have attached a letter to help you better understand my position. I tried on my last campus to do the right thing and go through the right channels. However, nothing happened. I ran to the promotion just to have people from the school call me with the same concerns.*

If we as a district can claim to take a stance about children bullied, can we not support those expected to protect them? I am emotionally drained from people who lacked the common decency to simply be kind. I am not leaving when I did not do anything to cause people to act in evil ways and have no regard for my well-being. I will face them daily if necessary and report every day of any abuse. I fully expect this district to care about all its employees and me. That's not too much to ask.

Later in the evening, Janie emailed twice, changing her investigative results to Marsala wine being baked into the cake, and pretended to be unable to spell Marsala correctly. The second response, after calling the bakery again, Kahlua and rum were baked into the cake.

Chapter 10

Love, Justice, Forgiveness

The day after Janie asked if I wanted to stay at the school, I walked into the main office to wash my coffee cup. In a narrow passageway in front of the sink stood Mandy, the area director, and a middle-aged, professionally dressed Hispanic man. When Mandy saw me, she enthusiastically introduced, "Mr. Jeremiah, this is our counselor, Darline McElroy!"

With spastic movements, he stated, "Oh, oh! You are an important person!"

The area director turned her face away from me after Mr. Jeremiah's comment. I suspected I had been the subject of private conversations. I responded, "Well, that's what some say."

Turning her face towards me, the area director then extended her hand, "Hi, I'm Bernadine Clark, the area director. I think I've seen you in a few meetings."

I shook her hand and refrained from sharing my thoughts. Area directors and counselors are not commonly in meetings together. Wearied of people's pretensions, I lost the ability to care. Shortly after, I discovered the reasons for her nervousness.

Mr. Jeremiah was very kind and often offered his assistance during his time at the school. The staff liked him as well. He sometimes stared during meetings where I needed his attendance as though he wanted to ask questions. Had he, I would have spoken for eternity because I needed the emotional outlet. He soon divulged he was a good friend of Bernadine Clark. He previously hired her as his assistant principal, Bernadine's first leadership role. Since he had retired, she often called him to substitute for principals when needed. I did not know his intentions for sharing the information, but I was grateful he shared it.

The school's atmosphere was as though we were all attending a funeral repast. Some shared happiness and the weight lifted by no more prolonged suffering under Brock's leadership. A co-worker, offended often by his sexual innuendos, came to my office, and expressed gratitude. A teacher blew kisses whenever she saw me. It is never my desire to receive accolades. Their heartfelt expressions and tears would have customarily encouraged me, but I needed an angel. I needed saving from the emotional burdens of it all. Deciding not to run was what I had to do, but not my desire.

Others were unhappy because Brock was gone. I understood it. He gave favors and leniency to specific teachers and frequently buying staff food and treats. His grooming reached into our pockets, eventually asking for money to purchase or bring food items. He scheduled the office staff to cover the teachers' lunch and recess duties periodically. Brock overrode the district's dress policies encouraging teachers to wear shorts, yoga pants, or athletic wear. They were victims as much as the child I reported to CPS.

Mandy was the happiest I had seen after Brock left. I did not know if she was trying to pretend everything was okay or assume Brock's role as the school's principal. In the following weeks, Mandy attempted to win over a few people she previously mistreated. Teachers shared she verbally reversed all the staff movements Brock made for the upcoming year. A few days later, the same teachers returned to me, confirming she did not have the authority to make those changes.

Initially, after the cake, Mandy greeted me as often as she saw me. Her greeting was loud and upbeat. She and Sally strutted through the hallways. Rumors of Sally and Mandy's involvement with the cake floated daily, with some people having the courage to ask. Though I needed to release the emotions by way of conversation, it was also very embarrassing.

I made it a point to only speak to Mandy, as necessary. We spoke during meetings she was required to attend, but that was the extent of our conversations. Mandy could not be trusted. I did not want her to take any of my words and used them for more retaliation as I thought everything was under investigation.

In earlier interactions, I stopped by the testing room on my way home one afternoon to ask if she needed help with testing administration. Mandy responded by asking why I burst into the room as though I was angry. I was confused at Mandy's response to my offer of assisting with a responsibility she frequently complained about doing. I also previously dismissed her comments regarding my natural hair. Coming into my office one day, she asked, "You braided your hair?"

Feeling awkward at the inflections and facial gestures, I answered to justify my hairstyle, "Yes, I don't want to cut it. I braided the sides of my hair as it is growing out."

She waved a hand with one finger pointing towards my hair and laughing, "What are you trying to do? Get a high top?"

After she left, I shared her comments in disbelief. I knew it was a racial insult but did not want to address it. I did not want others to think I was another Black person who had a chip on their shoulders by pulling the famous race card. I resisted the urge to attack her verbally, creating the same self-doubt she attempted to put in me. If I allowed the evil forces within her to pull me in, my testimony becomes tainted. Our real Enemy's goal is to force us into meaningless battles so that those who proclaim Christ reflect worldly images. Therefore, it weakens the message of Christ.

Before the cake incident, when I became quiet around Mandy, she visited my office, telling me she needed a calm spot. She often inquired what teachers said about the environment or administrators. Other times, she pretended to discuss biblical concepts and why she did not attend church. Her comments about other Christians she knew were not genuine, but I was the real deal was Mandy's way of degrading my beliefs. I did not realize until after the cake incident Mandy was the heathen, she often called herself.

The office staff shared their frustrations from Mandy's behavior, such as giving the White data clerk privileges. Some responsibilities assigned to the data clerk, Mandy, rerouted the duties to others. Mandy, often irritated by minor things, sometimes did not speak, but she was always friendly and respectful towards the data clerk.

Mandy also projected her beliefs on underprivileged children, which was mostly the school's population. She did not think the food program I oversaw for disadvantaged students to get weekend food was necessary. When I invited an autistic student to a Christmas party for underprivileged children, she ranted about the autistic students received twelve hundred dollars a month. Therefore, they did not need extra gifts.

Once, I explained to Mandy why I chose to help a teacher with an after-school Bible study. When I offered to help another teacher change classroom because of the large number of supplies, Mandy expressed her disapproval for both. Even when she often corrected me in meetings with parents, I let it go. I overlooked her behaviors and undermined my instinct. After all, my job position was to work as an administrative team with Mandy and Brock. I consistently tried to make sure what I experienced at the previous school did not influence my views or actions.

I was also concerned with looking as though I was the root of the conflict. Black women live and breathe under the stereotype of an angry Black woman regardless of the actions done to them. It is as though others' abusive actions become our responsibility to accept and pretend abuse does not hurt. Admitting hurt then subjects us to being labeled dramatic or ghetto. Whereas Mandy cried at work in the presence of others, my tears waited until safely at home. Mandy knew the system believed in her and would overlook whatever she had done. Suddenly, all her previous actions no longer existed.

Mandy's behaviors consistently indicated an inability to lead as well as living as a decent human being. For these reasons, I knew Mandy's crying to the nurse and district's investigator was as sincere as a child sneaking a favorite candy. Mandy had the privilege of skin color. One tear, one sob story, was all it took for Mandy's innocence. Her actions did not matter. It was my job to forgive and pretend everything was an accident: just smile and nod.

Along with my emotional pendulum came doubts of if I were doing the right thing by seeking justice. Christians are often faced with love thy neighbor so frequently we become martyrs to sin. The misunderstood ideas of love and forgiveness leave many as scapegoats that hinder healing as well as justice. I was often encouraged by well-meaning Christians to let it go and let God deal with those who decided to pervert justice. I was asked, "Aren't you treated nicely now?" as though the present behaviors remedy the injustices or breaking the law.

Many days I thought to bow out. However, when God places you on a path, there is a spiritual pull that will not allow you to release the assignment. I pushed out the concerns and fears that contradicted what I believed the Spirit led me to do. When you fully surrender your life, there is a spiritual drive that seeks God's will on earth. The Holy Ghost power enables the spiritual being to encourage the physical nature to deny self and put on Christ.

In more manageable tasks such as feeding the poor, visiting the sick, or giving money to various causes, we shout WWJD's famous slogan, What Would Jesus Do? When more difficult tasks come which requires faith, it is easier to cover under the misconception of love and forgiveness. Seldom do we hear the slogan WWJD when oppression is evident. We are more concerned with political agendas than those who should benefit from those agendas regarding racial and socioeconomic equity.

If we are not careful, we escape spiritual responsibility by imploring the need for peacemakers. Peacemakers are needed. However, we must understand the only time a peacemaker is required is during a conflict. No one needs water when water is available. As water resolves a drought, truth resolves a conflict. To wear the title peacemaker, we must step into a conflict and negotiate for peace through Godly resolutions. Godly solutions require truth.

Seeking justice can also appear to some as not having a forgiving heart. We understand forgiveness extends grace to no longer hold a sin against a person. Forgiveness protects the forgiver as well as the forgiven. The forgiver gradually or immediately releases emotions connected with the act committed against him or her.

Forgiveness is the expectation that the one forgiven would extend the same grace to the forgiver by acknowledging the sin or wrongdoing. The forgiven can release themselves from guilt and shame from the sin committed. It cannot be the reason the forgiver forgives. However, acknowledgment could be the catalyst for the forgiver releases the emotions and restores the relationship. If the forgiven cannot accept responsibility, it will create unhealthy cycles in the relationship.

Both the forgiver and the forgiven have a responsibility in the process. The perfect example of forgiveness in action is Jesus accepting punishment for the world's sins. Jesus freely offers forgiveness without payment. However, there is an expectation of the forgiven. The responsibility of the forgiven is more than just accepting forgiveness. Repentance is necessary. When accepting Christ's forgiveness, the forgiven acknowledges sin. If sin is not acknowledged, why is forgiveness needed? There is no need to come to Christ for a person who believes sin does not exist.

Repentance means the forgiven turns from sin and work to change the behaviors. No, works cannot pay for eternal life. A changed life is the result of the forgiven who truly accepts Christ's forgiveness. This change is the personal relationship where God peers into the heart. It is not up to the forgiver to determine if the forgiven is saved or not saved. But the fruit or actions may determine the level of trust in the relationship leading to authentic restoration.

Forgiveness and repentance must intertwine if the Christian is going to live a fruitful life. Often, Christians lock other Christians into abusive lifestyles because we teach forgiving others, but we neglect the teaching of repentance. We place the responsibility of forgiving seventy times seven on the forgiver but do not hold the forgiven accountable.

Accountability is not the same as unforgiveness. Accountability is holding oneself to a standard that does not consistently or intentionally harms another person. Forgiveness, in the absence of accountability, strains any relationship. While we cannot force others to repent, we can change how or if we interact with those who seek forgiveness without repentance or consistently break respectful boundaries.

The forgiver can decide to separate from the person without holding the sin against the forgiven. Often, parting from relationships is also frowned upon regardless of the toxicity.

Unfortunately, and wrongly, some believe forgiveness includes maintaining abusive relationships. This is not to say we should abandon every relationship where repentance is not evident. Change takes time. We look at the relationship's totality. Every relationship maintains balance from love, justice, and forgiveness.

There are two comparable accounts in how Jesus operated in love, justice, and forgiveness. Jesus' interaction with the woman at the well and the woman caught in adultery teaches us to love, desire justice, and forgiveness in action.

With the woman at the well, Jesus waited and initiated a conversation with her. She was not prepared to accept Him. He called out her sin, not to embarrass her, but to open her spiritual eyes to the truth of His identity. Calling out her sin was done in love as it was done in private and not with condemnation. Although Jesus judged her sins, He judged rightly and revealed the truth of Himself to her. He gave her life and an authentic purpose.

The woman caught in adultery was brought to Jesus. Like the woman at the well, she had what appeared to be a man problem. Instead of focusing on her sin, Jesus called the accusers to look in the mirror by saying one of the most famous scriptures, "He who is without sin, cast the first stone."

Her accusers attempted to follow their version of the law by stoning her for adultery. It was an unbalanced scale. Only the woman was brought to Jesus, whereas both should have by law (Leviticus 20:10). Jesus used this opportunity to teach a thought-provoking, self-reflective lesson and to execute fair judgment. God does not operate in injustices. But to this woman, he explicitly stated, "Go and sin no more." He did not condemn, but Jesus commanded her to change.

Both examples show an expression of love, justice, and forgiveness. Without justice, love does not exist. The Bible is transparent regarding love and justice. God is love, and God loves justice (1 John 4: 16, Isaiah 61:8 NIV). Justice cannot be applied correctly without love. Love rebukes so repentance can bring about God's desires, a relationship with Him through His son, Jesus.

Love also contemplates the situation before administering justice. When love and justice intertwine, it does its best work, restoration. Both women appeared to have a similar sin problem, but Jesus related the truth differently. To one, He allowed her to run into town and preach about Him. For the other, He commanded she stop sinning.

I struggled for many weeks. Did Brock and Mandy deserve love? Absolutely. Would it be a sin for me to hold or desire to hold them accountable for their actions? Were their actions against God? It is one thing for a person to hurt your feelings. However, if the action is a sin against God's Divine Will, we have the responsibility of righteous indignation. There is no sin in being thirsty or hungry for justice.

Sins against God will continue to perpetuate, causing harm to a multitude of people. To be used by God for His purposes, we must thirst and hunger for righteousness, not revenge. When a person decides to inflict emotional or physical pain, the person usually does not stop at one person. Sin seeks to devour and remains hungry.

Brock and Mandy's harassing and negligent behaviors put innocent children and adults in continuous harm. The more empowered by way of supportive upper administrators, the more those behaviors continued. Each emotionally damaged person then is at risk of inflicting pain on people within their circle. Most people do not realize where the real source of abuse lies, so those near and dear become the stress' recipients. If I allowed the effects from years of workplace abuse to rule over me, it would have potentially damaged five people, my family. Of course, it spreads through them in the years to come. This is how evil takes over.

Some think God will do the work eradicating abuse. Of course, God can instantly kill anyone who sins. If God took this method, there would be no one on earth. For all have sinned and fallen short of the glory of God (Romans 3:23 NKJV). God seeks to bring all to salvation, so He uses people as vessels to reach others. We are mediators of His will. Sometimes when the curtain of sin pulls back, sinners bow down to the only God who can save them. If we refuse to stand on Godly principals privately and publicly, we neglect to make disciples within our reach. We cannot make disciples by agreeing with sinful decisions.

There is a major difference between justice and retaliation. Seeking revenge is following your hurt instead of Godly principles. Revenge will not allow prayer to intercede for directions or solutions. Revenge seeks self-gratification and requires no faith. It refuses to listen to God; therefore, we do not have a right to revenge. Revenge is prideful. Pride assumes it can handle life without God. The Lord said the vengeance is mine (Deuteronomy 32:35, Romans 12:17-19 NKJV). We are not above God; therefore, we cannot exalt ourselves to take what belongs to Him. For example, if I decided to key Brock and Mandy's cars or break all the windows to their homes, it is a sin and against the law. I have then become just like the accused by plotting and committing evil.

It is impossible to wait on God's timing and instructions with a revengeful heart. Revenge creates a stubbornness in the believer. Once something becomes callous, the hardness rejects sound doctrine. Rejection of sound doctrine leads to ungodly passions (1 Timothy 4:3 NJKV). Our ungodly desires will encapsulate us in sin, and the Spirit of God cannot dwell in an unclean temple. Without the Holy Spirit, there is no guidance, no comfort, and no God within us (Romans 8:9 NKJV).

Love seeks justice through the avenue of forgiveness. The atmosphere of forgiveness guides and provides direction. In this atmosphere, we can pray and seek God's will instead of our own. While forgiveness is righteous, so is justice. It is a deception to believe seeking justice is a lack of love. God loves us, but He also corrects us (Hebrews 12:6, Proverbs 3:12, Psalms 94:12 NKJV). We are told to love justice, seek justice, and be just. It is a sin to justify the wicked and condemn the righteous (Proverbs 17:15 NKJV). When we do not answer the call to assist others, an unintended consequence is supporting the wicked.

Did Brock and Mandy, as well as their superiors, willfully reject justice? Was the sin or evil, one that, if not held accountable, would impact others? Would I fall to revenge if I sought fair and balanced treatment? Am I loving my neighbor? These are the questions I struggled to work through, primarily because of some responses.

Another well-known example of God correcting in the presence of love and forgiveness is the story of King David and Bathsheba, Uriah's wife. God dearly loved David. David was a man after His heart. David had a sexual relationship with Bathsheba and impregnated her. After his scheme failed to make her husband, Uriah, think the child was his, David ordered Uriah killed.

In David and Bathsheba's account, the prophet Nathan was told by God to address David's sin. David disregarded the seriousness of keeping God's commandments and gave God's enemies, unbelievers, the opportunity to ponder if perhaps this God of Israel was not who God's people claimed Him to be. Not only did God punish David, but He issued the consequences publicly and through David's heritage. God defended His character to remind believers and unbelievers He is righteous and just.

David fasted, prayed, and wept, hoping God would change His mind. His actions were not acceptable, so fasting, praying, and crying did not move God to allow David's sins to go unpunished. God operated in forgiveness as he allowed David to live and kept His covenant with David. However, God did not remove the consequences (2 Samuel 12:1-22 NKJV). We learn to continue to seek God's heart through prayer and fasting through David's sorrow. We do not give up but accept God's outcome.

God also did not allow Nathan to simply take the bystander approach, allowing the abuse of others. The bystander concept is a requirement our children in schools learn regarding bullying or mistreatment of others. If it is dangerous to intervene, children learn to find an adult to report the bullying. All too often, we give children responsibilities adults are afraid to own. There are many adult bystanders in our homes, churches, workplaces, and society. We see abuse of all kinds, but because it does not involve our loved ones or us, we turn a blind eye.

Nathan's task was arduous. David was a reputable warrior. Since we are to bear spiritual fruit, then we accept God's way of producing it. Nathan knew David's power and influence; however, the prophet Nathan obeyed God and corrected David. Yet, he followed God's command and approached David through a parable.

If God loves justice, but we refuse to apply justice righteously, what does this indicate in our relationship with God? Taking the passive approach will cost us blessings in every area of life. We will also have to face God's accountability. We are losing our very lives trying to save them by operating in fear or greed. We could eliminate the need for massive protests if we practiced love, justice, and forgiveness daily. We will not have the same paths in seeking justice, but we all will have the opportunity to exercise it.

Brock and Mandy were a fractional part of a more significant problem. Their actions just opened the platform for God could take care of the roots of the main issues. Again, this was not the first time I experienced racism and workplace harassment. It was not the first time injustice stood up and demanded attention. There are examples of ill-treatment through lack of promotions and disregard for higher-level Black administrators' authority. Placing Hispanic teachers only in bilingual classes as needed, and strategically manipulating circumstances against those unwanted to force resignations.

If we refuse to allow God to use us, then the world's problems will increase. When Christians refuse to use God's light, we also do not fulfill the command of making disciples in our homes or other facets of society. We are taking our light and hiding it under the bushel (Matthew 5:15 NKJV).

Unjust leadership decided Brock's behavior with a child was acceptable, and the retaliation against me was warranted. If this was not enough, they gave excuses for the actions or did not acknowledge wrongdoing in both incidences. Those who were supervisors of the area's director, human resource elementary manager, and the district investigator decided their positions were more important than the children and staff's well-being.

One may debate that a reprimand might have happened behind closed doors. However, when the area director received a district promotion and Brock gained a less accountable opportunity, it is unlikely a reprimand mattered. More than likely, my incident is not and will not be an isolated case. As Dr. Martin L. King stated, "Injustice anywhere is a threat to justice everywhere. We are caught in an inescapable network of mutuality, tied in a single garment of destiny. Whatever affects one directly, affects all indirectly."

As I toiled in prayer by the Spirit's prompting, I reminded myself often I was only the vessel. God is the jury, bailiff, court reporter, court usher, lawyers, and, most importantly, the Judge. I could only do what He requested. Thankfully, we do not possess all power to control the decisions and lives of others. However, we possess His spirit within us that empowers us to develop an understanding of God's will. Once we understand His will, we will operate in His power, creating the changes needed in society and our lives.

Chapter 11

"As I Have Loved You"

John 15:12

During the nine years in Lowland ISD, I did my best to follow God's lead and push aside emotions. Our feelings can be easy to follow but can also be expensive deficits. The day I resigned was just as turbulent as the day I started. I had to learn to let go after learning to stand still. As earthly wisdom suggests, we never quit a job before getting a job. However, I held on knowing it was time to depart. I finally accepted I needed to let go of what I considered security to hold hands with the faithful One. With God's grace, I had recently completed the requirements for professional counseling. Within a couple of weeks, I started interviewing and creating plans for my own business while completing this book. It was a period of tested faith in every turn. Thankfully, God has a way of escape when needed.

During Wednesday's night bible study, God gave me a new perspective on trials from a sixteen-year-old young man's prayer. He prayed, "Lord, thank you for trusting us with the problems we have in our lives." It had not occurred to me when God allows problems to come our way, He trusts us. Of course, at times, I did not want this amount of trust.

Spiritual stewardship is high stakes, for it usually involves more than the person seen in the storm. God uses our experiences or circumstances to impact more people than we often realize. Using the previous examples, more people than just the central person either benefited from or suffered because of their spiritual stewardship. David's choice with Bathsheba impacted two households severely for a lifetime. The woman at the well introduced others to Jesus, the Savior. Jesus' decision to live as an example and give up His life allows everyone who called on His name to have life and life more abundantly.

We cannot overlook the spiritual stewardship we have within our reach. We are not people's saviors, but God does expect us to exhibit neighborly responsibilities. It is not a handout to others but a hand up. It is a connection of spirits to His Spirit. According to His Divine grace, the Holy Spirit will guide us when and when not to be involved. If we choose fear over God's Spirit, urging us to answer the call, we will allow sin to reign and fail at Godly stewardship.

Early one morning, I was spiritually inclined to help someone else. Waking up in early morning hours between three and five o'clock became the norm to study, pray, or whatever the task placed on my heart. I resolved the timing as God's doing for specific purposes. When I completed what God placed on my heart during wait periods, I slept soundly through those early hours. April 25, 2019, compelled to write a letter on Mr. Rosario's behalf, I could not sleep. I tossed and turned and tried to pray myself back to sound slumber. Early mornings made long days. The longer I stayed in bed, the more the words for the letter continued in my head.

Mr. Rosario received an in-district transfer to another elementary school where Brock had befriended the principal. I knew Brock was still undermining Mr. Rosario as I recalled his behavior with Mr. Rosario's principal in a previous meeting. Mr. Rosario's principal would not recommend a contract renewal; therefore, Mr. Rosario planned to resign according to a mutual co-worker. I also recalled the number of times Brock said Mr. Rosario was not a good teacher. However, the former principal did not have the same concerns.

Brock's calendar was filled with meetings with Mr. Rosario when he taught at our school. The office staff was required by Brock to make our work calendars shareable to be viewed. Being occupied with my responsibilities, I did not think about Mr. Rosario's consistent meetings on Brock's calendar. My focus was Brock and Mandy's availability. I was responsible for scheduling parent meetings for students' academic and behavior interventions.

Mr. Rosario once wrote a letter to Brock, Mandy, and me. I was considered a part of the administrative team, so sometimes teachers included me when there were concerns. Again, I did not pay much attention to it because I was unaware of the entire situation. I tried not to get too involved with staffing concerns, which there were many as I was an emotional outlet for those who no longer trusted Brock and Mandy.

Brock, Mandy, and Sally often spoke ill of Mr. Rosario. Brock made jokes about him to the office staff, and Mandy did not like his personality. Mandy believed she had an advantage over Mr. Rosario, as she often stated that he needed his job to stay in the United States. Sally's preference was always Mandy's, so she often snubbed her nose at the thought of him. I did not concern myself with whether their actions were warranted. My focus was obedience to God's prompting.

Dragging myself up, I threw on my long light blue robe, stumbled into the kitchen for a strong cup of coffee, and went upstairs to my computer. All the words, sentences, and phrases flowed through the keyboard, releasing my head's tension. After writing, I returned to the kitchen to get a second cup of coffee. I needed to get dressed for work. I gave myself enough time to review the letter for errors, as I was sure to make while being half asleep. I waited until six o'clock to text him for his email address. He wondered why, and I told him to read the letter to answer his question.

His response floored me. *I truly appreciate your word(s) about me and respect the courage you show by putting it (in) written (form) and offering it to me to use it at my will. I can say you are not different from the image I have about you: a strong fair lady with deep beliefs and values. Thank you very much!*

The year before my CPS report, Mr. Rosario reported Brock for indecent behavior towards a child and intentionally blowing a bullhorn behind an autistic child after a fire drill. Brock was determined to destroy him by any means necessary with Mandy as his helper and support. Later, I learned he had given up on maintaining his career. The letter gave him the strength to try.

I did not see myself as courageous. It felt like the usual me, nothing special. I was just the same girl from Mississippi who refused to deny the truth. Searching for God through prayer and studying the Bible, I learned how God created us was intentional. Our personalities are for specific purposes within God's realm. Just like the disciples, we each are unique. Our goal is to allow God to develop us in the image of His Son, Jesus. We become more like Christ as we connect with God through Jesus to do the work assigned daily.

Before my husband's call to Pastor, I struggled to reconcile my self-perception compared to God's perception. From previous negative statements or following particular church culture practices, I placed futile expectations on myself. I eventually realized and acted upon that we are to use who we are for His glory. "For we are God's masterpiece. He created us anew in Christ Jesus, so we can do good things He planned for us long ago" (Ephesians 2:10 NLT). God did not use His time to create a person to simply focus on outward appearances or pretentious practices. If a big hat could successfully carry me through life, I would never remove it. The expectations of how a Pastor's wife acts and looks are so carnal minded that you must give up God to fulfill those expectations.

Once I realized this truth, it was liberating. The song produced by Kirk Franklin, "Imagine Me," resonated more than ever. It is imperative we love and free ourselves from expectations and live in the freedom of God. Otherwise, we will not be able to do Kingdom work for fear of ineffective expectations.

Because of our imperfections, God uses our experiences to teach us. Our spiritual growth is like the mutants of X-men. When we realize our gifts, talents, or faith level, we must learn to manage that power. We must develop in self-control, which always comes by seeking God about life-altering decisions. Otherwise, that same power becomes a curse instead of a blessing. As we grow, we give ourselves grace, but we strive to become good stewards of the power within us. We have this freedom in Christ because of Christ's redemptive power that saved us. We do not have to worry about salvation for those who believe in Christ are saved. This freedom allows us to bear the fruit of good works knowing mistakes will not strip away salvation. This freedom will enable us to honor God with our lives.

How could I possibly tell God I loved Him, but not love Mr. Rosario to give him what I believed could help? How do we as Christians decide it is okay to see our brother or sister mistreated, but allow fear to override the Spirit? How will we follow Christ's command to make disciples? How can God trust us with our requests for more, but ignore what He provides in the present? Is life more than just food and clothing? Will God not provide another whatever you need if you stand for righteousness? Can the same God who created the universe not make a path for us?

I was not one hundred percent positive about Brock and Mandy interfering with Mr. Rosario's career. Still, I decided now was the time to use what God puts in all His children, the Holy

Spirit as our guide. God operates on faith. If God promised the Holy Spirit would direct us, comfort us, and lead us, I decided to trust God. I would not make the same mistake I made in overlooking what I felt regarding Mandy's behaviors.

I knew it was risky. But what is not? We drive on dangerous highways and fly on planes with unknown pilots. We throw babies in the air for laughs, ride new rides at state fairs without knowing the engineers, and eat food without knowing the cooks. We trust many things and many people who we do not and possibly will never know. Indeed, we can trust the One Who is the Keeper of all. If I lost my job helping Mr. Rosario, it was time for me to leave the job. After all, it was God who gave me the position. What God gives, another cannot take unless God allows it. Whatever God allows, it is with a higher purpose. If God gets the glory, we should be satisfied.

After a few months, God was gracious in allowing me to know I had followed the right path. In a conversation with one of the teachers who had attended a job fair with Brock and Mandy, I told her everything I was experiencing within the district. When I mentioned Mr. Rosario's name, with visible disappointment, she stated, "That poor guy! After every table he went to for a job, the principal from the school would come to our table and ask Brock if that was the lazy teacher, he had told them about. He had no chance."

When Jesus stated, "A new command that I give you: Love one another. As I have loved you, so love one another," isn't a passive and conditional love. It is the very opposite. The way Jesus loved was in action, truth, Spirit, and reprimand when needed. If Jesus came to earth, walked around daily saying I love you, but refused to heal in various ways, fellowship, and not saved us from sins, no one would have known Him today. We know Jesus because of His purposeful living and saving grace.

Because of His selflessness, we can open ourselves to continue His work as gratitude.

Chapter 12

Persecuted, not Abandoned

It is incredible how we float through life to maintain routines. I knew my emotional health was in need. I coped mostly through prayer, music, Bible reading, and journaling. Balancing the CPS report's emotional toll, the retaliation, and my usual responsibilities were more challenging than I realized. Our minds and bodies will notify us when we need to stop and care for ourselves.

I did not know the enormous pressures I carried until one morning after a student came to my office. At her plight, I became angry and then cried. It was not the first time I had heard what she was sharing, so I knew I was not crying about her problem. I felt terrible about the emotional support she needed from me as a counselor and an adult was not available. I apologized and turned my back to compose myself several times. Her problem was severe, and I followed the protocol to help her after I finally stopped crying.

I called the district's crisis counselor to assist and emailed the counseling department coordinators to contact me. By happenstance, responding to my email was Olivia Martin, the same coordinator in the impromptu meeting with Janie Lang and Dr. Jennifer Starks. I left my office and went into a classroom for privacy to call Olivia. Immediately when she answered, I cried.

Since Olivia knew the reasons for my emotional breakdown, I did not have to waste time explaining it.

"Darline, you really need to take a few days off."

"I know, but I don't think I have any days left to take without getting docked." Any educator understood this as a couple of daily rates taken out of your check was significant. I was not usually concerned about missing pay in cases of emergencies or needed self-care. I needed to take time off, but I hesitated. I wanted to be stronger. Being docked from my pay check was just the excuse to stay and appear as tough as nails.

The counseling coordinator responded, "I can see if the counseling department can help with that, but I'm not certain. I am certain you need to go home for self-care."

I agreed and returned to my office to gather my things. The crisis counselor I previously called arrived and took care of the student while I talked with the counseling coordinator. She waited around to speak with me because I cried when I called her as well. We had a good relationship, and she was aware of the alcohol in the cake.

I discussed the recent events with her and showed her the final email from the district's investigator regarding the cake. As I inferred, Janie Lang supported Mandy. She disregarded the nurse's statements of the cake being the strongest dessert she had with alcohol and the fact the nurse once worked in a bakery. The day the Janie Lang referred to Mandy as remorseful, I knew the chances of her being objective and honest were out the window.

Responding to my question of who was at fault, she stated, *I'm not saying anyone is at fault. However, the bakery does not put stickers or any notations on their Tiramisu cakes, informing customers of alcohol baked into them. When I called back and asked specifically about the marsala wine, I spoke with the manager. She informed me there was no wine in the cake, but there were Kahlua and rum.*

As if that was not enough foolishness, she continued, "Mandy knew you didn't want a cake and said it was purchased because it had cookies around it. You confirmed you loved cookies."

Turning to the crisis counselor, I laughed and said, "How you just going to make me look greedy by saying I love cookies, and it's my fault basically!" By this time, I turned off the computer and had my work bag ready to leave.

The emotional break of laughter between us relieved some of the grief. It quickly ceased when the crisis counselor asked, "If Mandy knew you liked cookies, why not get cookies instead of a cake."

Memories resurfaced as my mind processed her words. "Yeah! One year the office staff purchased Tiff's Treats for my birthday. That's exactly what I'm going to tell her!" With that revelation, I turned on my computer to respond to Janie's email.

As the computer took its precious time, the counselor reveled in amusement that I turned the computer back on to send an email. "Girl, you are crazy!"

"I'm not crazy. I am tired! I'm tired of this foolishness as though it's acceptable to mistreat people. If this district wants a fight, then they got it. I may not win, but you are going to know that I've been here!" my Mississippian, Black Dog girl, emerged. From crying to ready to take on the world, I continued to wait for the computer to respond.

Empathizing, she shared, "I understand. I requested the surveillance videos once to prove my innocence in a situation."

I confided, "I requested videos, but I'm having a hard time with writing the request correctly."

"What are you talking about?" she asked, genuinely confused at my response to writing a request. I asked the principal, and he had them emailed to me within the same day or at least the next day."

Shaking my head, I responded, "Girl, they are giving me the run-around. I need an attorney."

She continued, "God is using you. I have often told you that I did not experience half of what you are experiencing, even with the workload. God has something for you to do here."

The computer finally came to life. Looking like a Kermit, the Frog meme, I read aloud as I typed my response. I noticed Janie Lang included her supervisor in the email, which added to my frustration. I typed, *Thank you for the response. You are right. I enjoy cookies, which is why she could have ordered Tiff's Treats as done in the past, but I guess that would have been too difficult to add alcohol of that volume.*

Shutting down things again while my friend laughed, we discussed racism within the district and her experiences. We walked out of my office. Mandy, Mr. Jeremiah, and a couple of school resource officers were in the hallway, resolving an issue. I went over to the group to tell Mr. Jeremiah I was leaving for the day. From the redness of my eyes and nose, it was apparent I had been emotional. Mandy smiled at me. She did not realize how much God loved her at that moment for someone who appeared to have a problem with Him.

You never understand the weight of what you are going through, especially if you do not have the choice but to continue through it. My experiences were challenging, not merely for what the leaders were doing. It was the most challenging because I was determined to follow God and not my emotions.

In past experiences, I was vocal, with no restraints on my opinions. I decided on what path or battle I engaged with others. If I wanted to leave a job, I went. Prayer came after my actions and not as a guide. If it was the wrong decision, then I prayed for God to release me. The idea of praying before a decision was almost obsolete.

Then there were my expectations of God that needed surrendering. Learning and waiting for God's instructions was the main struggle. I had years of maintaining self-centered habits that needed daily submission to God's authority. Also, I had to accept whatever outcome God wanted. Our obedience to God cannot demand God give us what we want. God is not the fictitious Santa Claus. There is no such thing as being good or bad; there is practicing righteousness or evil. We cannot tell God, okay, I have not committed fornication, now, give me a spouse or I did what you asked, so now I am ready to win the lottery. We do not always get what we desire, which is good.

We do not see the entire puzzle, just a piece or two, if that. Trusting God with the consequences is necessary for faith. If we decided the outcomes, there would not be a need for God. And what a terrible life we would all have if people determined the results for each other's lives.

Attempting to renew my mind, I repeatedly stated, "Lord, Your will be done." Yes, I wanted to curse Mandy, Sally, and punch the lights out of Brock. Janie Lang protected them for the wrong reasons. My life did not matter to any of them. Nevertheless, I desired that my choices reflected my heart. My heart is what God judges. When He investigates my heart, I want God to "create in me a clean heart and renew a loyal spirit within me" (Psalm 51:10 NKJV). God will only do in us what we allow Him to complete. A life that relies on what God calls sin for fulfillment rejects God's willingness to live in us.

Loyalty to God is to be what the world called "ride or die." There is only One I am willing to carry the label, "ride or die," who is Jesus. We must push away our desire to control the outcomes and submit to God's will. We trust His word as promised, "We know that all things work together for good for them who love God and to them called according to His purposes" (Romans 8:28 NKJV).

Yes, even the trickery and mockery from eating an alcohol-laced cake would work out for my good and those involved for His purposes. Many days I suffered to believe, but I believed enough to allow God to order my steps.

Chapter 13

Truth Revealed

The crisis counselor and I briefly chatted before I left the school. I came home around noon, grabbed a cup of green tea, and headed upstairs. I immediately searched for lawyers to take my case as it was apparent Janie Lang decided Mandy and Brock were benevolent. I reached out to several friends for references, with one being the NAACP. A friend texted an attorney reference with a teacher's organization. I initially did not want an attorney paid by a teacher's organization because I believe the attorneys worked more with the school system than the client. Since this was workplace harassment and discrimination, my second time within this school district, I did not want business as usual.

Attempting to obtain the videos through the Public of Information Act (PIA), I researched how to write the request. I copied and pasted from the internet as I waited on other attorney referrals to inquire for representation. The videos would prove everything I said to the district's investigator Brock, Mandy, and Sally had full knowledge of alcohol being in the cake. Of course, my language was less than amateurish, causing more delay to the district's advantage. Not knowledgeable of how to submit a detailed request, I omitted specifics according to the district's legal team representatives. I rewrote the request making corrections as best as I could.

I decided to use an attorney referral from the teacher's association. My dues paid into the teacher's association would cover the fees. To both Mr. Rosario and my surprise, the same lawyer representing him was my referral. Mr. Rosario called to get a better understanding of how I connected with his attorney, Attorney Miller. The attorney also requested Mr. Rosario relay information regarding a form to return, committing to his services. I felt a little uneasy that an attorney asked another client to speak on his behalf for paperwork.

I signed with the same attorney Mr. Rosario retained for his legal representation to strengthen his case. He had officially resigned under pressure but was completing his contractual time, the end of the school year. I believed God desired for me to assist him. I sent the attorney the information I requested from the district for his records. Attorney Miller informed he would also send a general request for additional records.

During the first two days of staying home, I organized paperwork and wrote a timeline of events to give to Attorney Miller. I spent a considerable amount of time praying and reading the Bible seeking direction. On the third day after leaving work early, my plans to return to work halted. I did not make it halfway from my house before I wept uncontrollably. I called my husband, telling him I could not go in. Confused as to why I was unusually emotional, I turned around and went home. I had no other choice but to call for a professional counselor. Something was very wrong; I was not bouncing back to my normal. I warred between resigning immediately and following God's will.

Lying in bed that evening, I stared at the ceiling, talking with God. It was the end of the month and the eve of payday. I expected my paycheck would take a hit for missing three days. Like Gideon, I needed reassurance. *God, if I am doing the right thing and have an authentic case against the district, allow all the money to remain in the check. If my pay is less than usual, I will know this is not*

Your desire to continue. Perhaps this was a faithless prayer, but it was all I had.

The next day, there was not one single penny missing from my pay. I returned to work the following week, knowing it was God's plan.

In the second week of Brock's removal from campus, an incredible sense of urgency flooded my mind to send a formal, written grievance to John Lee, the human resource elementary director. Again, I retreated to an upstairs bedroom. Since the elementary human resource director did not send the grievance form, I called a teacher who had recently sent a grievance against Brock to explain the process. After getting directions, I erased her information and added mine.

I watched the sunset as I read the school board's policies and federal laws of alleged violation citing examples of each. I knew it was late, but I could not stop until I completed the task. I ensured the first policy I listed for Brock was an educator should be of a good moral character using the CPS referral as support. Because the district investigator never mentioned what I reported was inaccurate, I firmly believed what I witnessed between Brock and the child.

I wanted to be thoughtful of mine and the district's best interests when asked to describe a remedy for the complaint. I knew from others' experiences in the district leadership could use revamping. It was just the beginning of my knowledge of how desperately leadership needed changes. My only goal was to see a difference in how leaders treated those they were accountable for serving. The few Black employees in various roles in the district shared racial disparities amongst staff and students.

By the time I completed the grievances, collected supporting documents, and scanned and emailed all the forms, my family was asleep. It was a grueling night between completing the forms, preparing for the next day, and switching my mind to resting mode. As usual, I prayed while reminding myself of Moses, Noah, and Esther. It was not easy for them, but the labored results provided hope and freedom for many.

The next morning, Sally put in my school's mailbox a letter that she would no longer assist me in giving computerized assessments to the students. I scanned and emailed the note requesting to attached it to Mandy's grievance. Mandy's grievance listed preferential treatment for Sally and its impact on school employees. Sally's note gave evidence of entitlement and retaliation.

Sally kept her word. During testing sessions with kinder and first grade students, which is the most difficult, Sally left. She dashed in and out the main office to tell the office staff how I struggled. Another co-worker advised me to call her district's department and request help. It was enough to bring her back to do her job. Sally later commented what was happening at the school was my fault, and I needed to let go of that "damn cake." She failed to realize it was not about the cake, and probably still believes in her heart it was my responsibility to accept their harassment.

The notice of Brock's return and not returning came the next day after sending the grievance forms. During dismissal, confusion and panic wreaked the atmosphere. Consecutively, people approached me with the news of Brock's return. For two weeks, many were in peace for the first time since the two years he had been there. In disbelief, people cursed, cried, and complained of the district's disregard of the school's climate. A short email from the interim principal I had not yet seen stated, *Great news-Brock will be back tomorrow!*

Standing at my office door for dismissal hall duty, I had a clear view the main office through the glass window. Sally paced near Mandy's office, and Mandy gleamed. Mandy previously told several people Brock would return, and she was sure of it. Those of us who did not want his return did not believe it was possible and dismissed Mandy as hopeful. Before I could get through the hallway to my car in the parking lot, another staff member approached me, stating that perhaps Brock was not returning. The interim principal received a phone call soon after sending the email to hold the announcement.

No one from the district gave any reasons for his removal from campus. The district's irresponsible actions left the teachers and front office staff to shoulder the parents' many questions. It was not until a teacher requested information from the area director after parents consistently asked various staff members. Then a general letter was sent to parents. Brock was only off-campus from the contents of the letter until after school dismissed for the summer.

Within a few days, a level two grievance was scheduled with Bernadine Clark, the area director. The Hispanic teacher, who previously encouraged me to call the news channels, had not received her meeting request. However, her grievance was filed weeks before mine. So quickly scheduled, the meeting did not allow me to meet with Attorney Miller physically. We realized the district needed to meet for their interest promptly. At my request, Attorney Miller postponed the meeting because the district had not given the requested Public Information.

After rounds of emails from the district attempting to withhold the PIA request, Attorney Miller threatened to contact the Texas Attorney General's office. The district finally sent the information except for the videos the weekend before Memorial Day. Attorney Miller sent them to me requesting I find supporting evidence for workplace harassment. I considered the request as unusual to look through the documents and determine what was helpful. Still, I complied, adding another task to my lifestyle.

Attorney Miller also forwarded me an email regarding the videos. The district's paralegal requested I come the same day at noon to view the videos. The district's paralegal bolded the word "not" in the phrase to add emphasis and the district's stance on releasing the tapes. Attorney Miller could not come because of his schedule but told me to view them alone. Since I was at work with a schedule of my own and believed this was not the step to take, I asked to reschedule so that my attorney could be present. Attorney Miller suggested we meet before the rescheduled level two meeting. Later, he emailed he could not make that appointed time either.

A couple of weeks later, Mandy announced her new assignment at an elementary magnet school. In the grievance, I requested Mandy's removal as soon as possible. Mandy bragged about her placement being a promotion since the school was a magnet school. Our school was a grade letter D from the state. She stopped speaking after the transfer announcement of leaving at the end of the school year. It was a blessing as I grew weary of smirking smiles when she spoke.

One of the office workers consistently encouraged me that Mandy was just another unhappy person seeking to bring her misery on others. From a philosophical viewpoint, I understood. Emotionally, I did not care.

Someone in the upper administration responded to my grievances without a formal meeting, which confirmed Brock's allowance to stay on campus and retaliate was negligence. However, I had no idea how negligent until I opened the attorney's email after arriving home. Having the opportunity to open the 194-page attachment from the district, I sat at the dining table while on the phone with my sister. I began to scroll and skim the document.

"Oh, my God!"

My sister, alarmed at my interruption of conversation, replied, "What? What is going on?"

"I can't believe what I am seeing! This has to be a mistake."

"What? What is it?"

"They didn't investigate him. Mandy knew all along about the CPS referral. Oh my gosh! They met with the parents of the child I referred to CPS and manipulated them."

In the PIA was an email Brock sent to upper administration regarding a meeting with the parents. Reading Brock's email sent to Dr. John Lee, Bernadine Clark, and Janie Lang, I was appalled at deceit, manipulation, and the support Brock and Mandy received. Brock had the unmitigated gall to suggest the child's parents, who I sought to protect, called the person who had made the report a "monster." He also stated that the parents wanted to speak with someone in the district for more information.

An email sent from the district's investigator, Janie Lang, confirmed Brock was good friends with John Lee, the elementary human resource director. Janie Lang used casual language in asking for the CPS worker's information to which she only received a name but no phone or badge number. Brock's statement to the incident was long with obvious excuses as to why he did not remove the child. Brock had the exact timing of the video recording. He sent emails he initiated to the child's teacher to back his story.

Having a massive tension headache, I got off the phone with my sister to take a rest. Afterward, I retreated to the typical upstairs bedroom, which was unused since my daughter was in college. I continued to read, saving the large, unorganized document to my file. There were no words to describe my feelings. Discouragement set in as I thought about the many staff developments, we discussed federal laws. The threat of losing your job loomed over you if you did not follow suspected child abuse protocol. I thought about how often I had stressed those words to the staff as directed by the counseling department. They were empty words with certain people who had an advantage over the laws. The abuse I experienced was expected and known, and no one cared.

Memorial Day weekend I spent crafting a letter to the district. I decided to use a similar format as the district's investigator exposing Brock and Mandy's retaliation and harassment regarding the Tiramisu cake. I included the information about the CPS report and how Brock and Mandy's supervisors protected them.

Disheartened by every piece of evidence I saw, I believed it was best to give those in leadership the opportunity to correct the wrongdoings. I hoped my time spent would move the needle for justice. With the feeling that I did not complete what I knew was wrong at the previous school, I persevered through the weekend revising and editing as best I could without anyone reviewing for mistakes.

I did not tell anyone what I was doing until after I sent the letter. I did not need the distraction or hesitation. May 27, 2019, after four days of sifting through 194 pages, I emailed a nine-page letter to the district's leadership, citing workplace harassment, hostile work environment, and institutional racism against Brock Lyles, Mandy Bloom, Bernadine Clark, John Lee, and Janie Lang.

Chapter 14

The Letter

May 27, 2019

Dr. William Glacier,

"Institutional racism is the process in which racial oppression is imposed on subordinate racial groups by dominant racial groups through institutional channels." (Encyclopedia.com)

After getting over obstacles of receiving Open Records from the Lowland ISD's general counsel, I was able to view and unfortunately discover that several employees deemed as my leaders had used their racial dominance to give an unequal power and advantages to Brock Lyles, principal, and Mandy Bloom, assistant principal thus creating a hostile work environment.

May 22, 2019, my legal representative, Mr. Leland Miller, requested that I view the Open Records attachment to see if any of it was important in supporting my grievances (see attachments 1 and 2) received on Tuesday, April 30, 2019, by John Lee, Elementary HR Director of LISD.

I discovered the following acts that led to a hostile work environment highly supported by Janie Lang, District HR investigator, John Lee, Elementary HR Director, and Bernadine Clark, District Area Director. Using the frivolous and unorganized 194-page document, the following are my findings:

August 22, 2018 email from the counselor, Darline McElroy to former Counseling Director and Dr. William Glacier, LISD Superintendent forwarded to Dr. Hodge Lackey, former asst. superintendent (p. 1 LISD; District P. 059)

- Reporting that a CPS report was made against an employee. Dr. William Glacier calls. I inform him of the details of the incident and a previous incident at Blue Valley's Middle School which makes me very reluctant to return to Freedom Elementary School in fear of retaliation. When the superintendent asked if there were other things that would indicate Brock Lyles's character, I responded that on two different occasions, Brock stated in SST meetings in the presence of parents that he considered 3rd-grade students as "virgin test takers because they had never done it before."
- I informed Dr. Glacier, LISD Superintendent, that Brock would know that I reported the incident as it was only the student, Brock, and myself involved in the incident. I explained that I feared retaliation because of Brock Lyles' behavior with Mr. Rosario after Mr. Rosario made a report on Brock Lyles having an inappropriate body reaction while looking at a child. Mr. Rosario is no longer at Freedom Elementary School because of his grievance of a hostile work environment.

August 24, 2018 email from Brock Lyles to Janie Lang

- Brock Lyles gives his statement to the District Investigator, Janie Lang, indicating that he was assisting the counselor with the student of the CPS investigation. **(p.133; LISD District pp. 190, 191)**

Saturday, August 25, 2018, email from Brock Lyles to the elementary director, Janie Lang, Bernadine Clark, and Dr.

Hodge Lackey, former asst. superintendent). (pp 135-136; LISD District 193)

- Brock Lyles requests a meeting with all. Bob Roberts on Monday, August 27, 2018, is the only district official who redirects Brock Lyles and reminds him that personnel matters and investigations are confidential.

September 6, 2018 email to the elementary director, Janie Lang, and Bernadine Clark (P. 7, LISD District 066)

- Brock Lyles and Mandy Bloom held a meeting with the parents of the child in which was the victim in the CPS report,
- Brock stated that he **had not been** contacted by CPS
- Brock stated that the parent considered the person reporting the incident a "monster" and expressed anger and frustration with the person who filed the complaint and wanted to speak with **district officials** which indicates that **no one from LISD** had spoken with the parents concerning the CPS report on August 22, 2018.
- Brock stated that the parents acknowledge that their child had communication difficulties and understood the child's "hugging" behaviors. However, several times with the teacher, (teacher of the child in the CPS report), and once with me in a meeting, the parents did not acknowledge any concerns for the child other than needing time to adjust and mature. Later, January 30, 2019, Brock Lyles blocked me from an SST meeting stating that the parents did not want me there with no explanation of why (see documentation with grievances) with the parents to attempt to have the child evaluated for speech. (documentation at Freedom Elementary School) They refused and humiliated the teacher as Brock sat in the meeting with no support to the teacher reported to me by

the therapist the day of the meeting and the teacher, (teacher of the child in the CPS report) days later.

- No one in the email reprimands Brock Lyles for speaking with the parents during an ongoing investigation in which **he is the perpetrator** or not informing the parents that whoever reported the incident was following the law as well as district responsibilities. The area director, Bernadine Clark even clarifies Brock's statement to Janie Lang by rewriting what Brock stated, therefore, validating his actions. John Lee, elementary director, and Janie Lang, district investigator, do not reprimand the meeting again supporting Brock Lyles and Mandy Bloom.

- In the confidentiality statements which staff members (pp.151-153) were told to sign in reference to Mr. Rosario's report, Brock Lyles and Mandy Bloom would be in violation of speaking with the parents whose child is part of the investigation as well as Brock Lyles especially since **Brock Lyles is the alleged perpetrator**. Also notice that Brock Lyles, Mandy Bloom, and Leo Tide do not have confidentiality statements signed, although Janie Lang was informed to have all sign confidentiality statements by the former asst. superintendent. **(p. 150, LISD District 208)**

- Janie Lang is given the timestamps of the video for the incident reported to CPS; **however, there is no documentation given in any of the records. (pp.5-6; LISD District 063-064)**

Friday, September 7, 2018 email exchange between Brock Lyles, elementary director, and forwarded to Janie Lang.

- Brock sends the name of the CPS caseworker. John Lee, elementary director, requested a status report. **(p. 137; LISD District 195)** (status report not included in PIA received)

140

Tuesday, September 11, 2018 email from Janie Lang to Brock Lyles and Mandy Bloom (P. 137; LISD District 068-069)

- In a very friendly exchange, Janie Lang requests the phone number of the CPS investigator; Brock tells Mandy to get the number and that he sends a copy of the badge. (no **documentation received in records request of phone number or badge**)

Saturday, February 9, 2019 email from the school nurse, Kia Leos to Janie Lang (p. 181, LISD District 239)

- Reports student being locked in the office with Brock Lyles

Monday, February 11, 2019 email from Janie Lang to Hope Nanez, Chief Leadership Officer

- Janie Lang asks Hope Nanez to clarify her role from the forwarded email from the school nurse. Tells Nanez that John Lee, Elementary HR Director, is good friends with Brock Lyles **(p. 181, LISD p. 239)**

End of any documentation on the CPS report. No formal report was given by Janie Lang.

Conclusion:

Brock Lyles was supported by Bernadine Clark, John Lee, and Janie Lang to stay on campus disregarding any possibilities of subjecting children to harm. No records indicating that security was informed of the CPS report from the counselor. No records giving a description of what happened in the video. No records on whether the counselor's report or Brock's report was factual. Brock Lyles, the alleged perpetrator could have a meeting with the parents who are from another country and whose dominant language appears not to be English prior to CPS contacting him and during the district's pseudo investigation. The teacher of the student nor the parents were never interviewed or informed by district officials per documentation received. No formal reports on either CPS case or the nurse's report, just notes. Bernadine Clark, elementary director, and Janie Lang do not inform Darline McElroy or Kia Leos to file formal grievances or the procedures in filing grievances if the employees believed policies and laws were being violated on either report of Brock Lyles's behaviors.

Later a report was made by Darline McElroy that Mandy Bloom purchased a cake with alcohol for my birthday. Using the 194-page document, here are the findings:

Monday, April 22, 2019, from Darline McElroy to Janie Lang (p. 43, LISD District 101)

- The email explains cake incident (no records of speaking with coworker mentioned in this report)

Notes from my report given to Janie Lang (p. 49; LISD District 107)

- Janie Lang was verbally informed of Sally's comments during lunch hour the day the cake was given, and in the written document (p. 43); Janie Lang did not write these comments on my report nor did she interview Sally per documentation. However, Sally came to my office the following day to explain why she called the cake "special".

Notes from nurse report, Kia Leos, given to Janie Lang (p.51; LISD District 109)

- Nurse's statement, "strongest alcohol tasting cake ever tasted"
- Nurse's statement, "worked in a bakery, definitely alcohol in the cake"
- Janie Lang notes, "called the bakery, no alcohol; read ingredients to me"

Notes from Mandy Bloom, Assistant Principal, given to Janie Lang (p.50; LISD District 108)

- Mandy states, "Brock ask if there was alcohol in the cake"
- Why, unless alcohol was strong enough to taste?
- Mandy states, "kick this year, wouldn't have anything to do with Brock" referring to Darline McElroy
  - Mandy asked me several times over the year, "what's up with you and Brock?" Once even stated in the presence of the office secretary, when I refused to order food Brock was purchasing for lunch, "She (Darline) doesn't want anything from Brock." However, Mandy knew exactly what the problem was as records indicated that she sat in on a meeting with Brock and the parents of the child reported in the CPS case on Sept. 6, 2018. **(p.7; LISD District 065)**
- baby shower being given as an example. The same baby shower where Brock humiliates me in front of several staff members referring to the alcohol in the cake by saying the punch was "Tiramisu punch". The same baby shower where Mandy sits by Sally saying, "stop and that she would next time purchase a cake from Sam's".
- Mandy stated, "Brock asked if alcohol were in the cake after 2-3 bites"; "I said out loud I would never do that." No one reports hearing this as Janie Lang does not interview with the other people in the office, office aide, office secretary, sub for office data clerk. (no records indicate interviews and I was verbally told by the office aide that they were never asked
- Bottom of Janie's report: Brock' denies the alcohol statement, but stated that the cake tasted "funky" (LISD **District 108)**

- o Brock a few minutes after leaving the office sends an email to all office staff including the SRO, "Can you get drunk off tiramisu cake?" **(p.44; LISD District 102)**

The attached grievances will give other information and documentation on the cake incident including how Janie Lang's "findings" are very inconsistent and only admits alcohol being "baked" into the cake **after** I requested videos. She later stated that Mandy Bloom did not knowingly purchase a cake with alcohol without requesting documentation from the uptown bakery, San Martin in Dallas, Tx. Her language, "Mandy purchased you a cake because you love cookies and you confirmed that you liked cookies," indicated her biases in the investigation and supporting Mandy whom she said was "very remorseful" in the meeting with Jennifer Starks, interim director, Olivia Martin, and myself. Mandy's comment on Janie Lang's documentation, "No one forced her to eat the cake," does not qualify as being remorseful.

Looking at Janie Lang's conclusive findings (pp.63-65, LISD District 101)

- Stated, I said Mr. Lyles's leg was grabbed-not in my report **(p.4)**
- Mr. Lyles admits to hand gestures and offensive comments but is once again concluded as "joking" (analysis and conclusion **p.65; LISD District 101)** and is told to act professionally with staff members.
  - o In meeting with Jennifer Starks, Interim Counseling Director, Janie Lang, Olivia Martin, Counseling Coordinator the following statements are made in response to CPS case and cake incident.
    - After Jennifer Starks is told of a previous CPS incident and cake incident; Jennifer Starks to Janie Lang, **"This is harassment! What are y'all going to do about him?"**

144

- Jennifer Starks to Darline McElroy, "I suggest you transfer. I have never seen anyone go this far out of the way to hurt someone. This is for your safety."
- Olivia Martin after I stated that I did not want to run anymore from problems and I wasn't the one in the wrong, **"Yeah! It's like the bully wins!"**
- Janie Lang slamming closed her notebook, "I'm tired of him! I have told him over and over again to watch his words."
- After Jennifer Starks and Olivia Martin leave the office, Janie Lang to Darline McElroy, **"Do you really want to stay at this school? I will talk to the upper admin."**
- Brock is off the campus from April 24, 2019, to April 30, 2019. Retired principal, Rod Jeremiah, is brought in to serve as principal.
- **April 30, 2019,** an email from Rod Jeremiah was sent about Brock returning the same day I was notified of my grievances received by elementary director early morning.
- **May 1, 2019,** an email was sent with a change of plans by Rod Jeremiah.
- **May 15, 2019,** Bernadine Clark sends a letter about Brock Lyles not returning prior to summer break to be given to students.

- Janie Lang's report disregards the nurse's reports on alcohol. A nurse who is trained and trusted by the district to give children all types of medication/drugs.
- Janie Lang's report does not include all who were in the office

- Janie Lang's report does not include any written documentation from the bakery including the actual cake order or receipts.
- Janie Lang's report indicates that she views the video footage, but only describes my actions while eating the cake. No actions of the others before nor after nor does she report on the video footage I requested outside of the office when Mandy and Sally walked out.
- Janie Lang's report does not include why Brock Lyles was to return to campus but later not return.
- Janie Lang's report disregards the discrepancies in Brock's statements compared to Mandy's statements on the alcohol being in the cake and Mandy's response to the incident.
- Throughout the investigation, Janie Lang includes John Lee, elementary director, in emails having full knowledge that "John Lee, elementary director, is close to Brock" as she mentions in the earlier investigation in the nurse's report of Brock locked in the office with students.

In conclusion, it appears that Janie Lang, John Lee, and Bernadine Clark, used their positions to give advantages to Brock Lyles and Mandy Bloom to exercise oppressive behaviors, violate district and legal policies, and behave in unprofessional manners disregarding the many reports given.

If this were an isolated incident, I could easily forgive and move forward. However, and unfortunately, this is not. In my email to Jennifer Starks, Janie Lang, and Olivia Martin following our impromptu meeting held earlier, I stated my reasons as to why I would not leave the campus. I attached an email from former area director in 2016 where I was the subject once again of racial discrimination and workplace harassment. Under the principalship of Blue Valley's Middle School principal, who used her assistant principals to high surveillance me and once included a reading specialist, I suffered emotional abuse from once again a hostile work environment.

Racism appears to be so commonplace in Lowland ISD that an area director can publish in an email acknowledging "racial concerns and needed new practices" but summed up the meeting as "it is what it is". She commends my honesty and courage, but not once guides me to file a formal grievance as she knows this behavior is against federal law. I receive "a pat on the back" and am told to try to transfer to Antioch Middle School, a school that is well known to have a higher percentage of Black staff and most often Black leadership.

Racism appears to be so commonplace in Lowland ISD that the district investigator seeks guidance on the White nurse's report of possible abuse prior to her investigation but disregards my CPS report and allows the principal to meet with the child's parents.

Racism appears to be so commonplace in LISD that two white leaders, Brock Lyles and Mandy Bloom can give a different report on breaking policies by bringing alcohol to campus, laughing about it while risking the life of a coworker as they had no knowledge of the coworker's health; yet, stay on campus to continue the abuse.

Racism appears to be so commonplace in LISD that a Hispanic teacher, Mr. Rosario is oppressed by two white leaders, Brock Lyles, and Mandy Bloom, while noted by many staff members as a good teacher with great classroom management and whom parents and students loved. Mr. Rosario once even mentored a student from a regular education classroom allowing the student to come into his bilingual classroom as the student needed a male role model. Mr. Rosario sought the help of upper administration but found himself having to transfer while a white teacher, Mia Glover, who I like personally, is given support and coaching to improve.

Racism appears to be so commonplace in Lowland ISD that a Black principal, James Williams, is removed from his campus during the investigation and eventually forced to resign for alleged testing irregularities while a white principal, Brock Lyles, remains on campus after a CPS report is given. Not only does he remain on campus but is given the opportunity to talk with the parents of the child. Perhaps because the child was Black, the state test was more important and needed protection.

Racism appears to be so commonplace in Lowland ISD that this Black woman fears continuous retaliation and cannot leave the district if she considers leaving because her leaders cannot be references for her job performances. A career in which she earned a distinguished award and acknowledged by the district. A career that she has received notes from students and staff acknowledging her willingness to help, support, and work diligently. A career where she spent 14 years in the classroom while attending graduate school as a wife and mother.

I have questioned why this same situation has fallen in my hands. I realize that I am responsible for how I deal with it. The first time, I walked away forgiving those who attempted to make life difficult for me. I rose above the hatred and obtained a school counselor's position.

It would be professionally irresponsible and against my values and morals for me to continue to allow people to be oppressive without attempting to report such incidences. It would also be morally and legally irresponsible to put children in a position of possible harm. Since I have no documentation of a full investigation being completed and the principal and assistant principal were given the opportunity to meet with the parents whose child was reported as being violated, I can only conclude that my findings are correct.

I have decided to not have the grievance meeting scheduled on Thursday, May 30, 2019, as it would be a waste of time, a disgrace to me, to sit in a meeting with an area director who has already decided that I'm not worthy of her professional judgment. It is obvious to me, given the reports I have received, that Brock Lyles and Mandy Bloom have her full support.

When I sat in the car of Dr. Grace Brentwood, former area director in 2016 in the parking lot of Highland Meadows Professional Building reporting the leadership at Blues Valley Middle School, I told her that I didn't want to be the additional voice of racism in a country already not united. The truth is that I am not the voice of racism. I am the recipient of racism and the voice that is calling out to balance the scales. Being Black in America does not qualify as a disability, so as a counselor I cannot write a 504 plan to give Black people equal rights and protection in Lowland ISD. It must be up to our entrusted leadership.

Respectfully submitted,

Darline McElroy

School Counselor

Chapter 15

Lonely, not Alone

Attorney Miller called early the next morning. "Am I your attorney? I had no idea you were going to send a letter to the district!"

"I'm aware you didn't know. All the information in the records revealed what I wrote. It's what I had to do."

"Am I still your attorney?"

"I need a few days. I may need to find a civil rights attorney. Do you have experience in that area?"

"Well, some."

I needed a more definitive response or a referral. I understood the curveball was unexpected but hesitating on your experience is not comforting. "I'm sorry if I have offended you, but I can't allow this to continue with this district. Please give me a couple of days to contact you regarding whether or not we should continue."

I honestly did not expect as much anger from Attorney Miller. We both previously responded to the district's attorney. He not once asked or advised me to allow him only to correspond with the district.

During our consultation, he advised that he talked during the level two meeting with the district. He would prompt me to express my feelings at the end. Attorney Miller knew my main reason for retaining him was for Mr. Rosario's case. Besides, I had previously asked Attorney Miller about suing the district twice. Both times he said the school districts' employees and officials qualified for legal immunity. The second time, stating, "I thought I told you this," turned my trust away. Although I was inexperienced with the law, I was not a child. Starting a sentence with "I thought I told you," is degrading unless you end the sentence with "there's a dessert, or you have an extra check in the mail."

I was not drinking Attorney Miller's unflavored colored water. There was no way in the devil someone could be reported to CPS, retaliate, harass, and risk a co-worker's life with a drug without legal accountability. Since Mandy knew I did not drink alcohol, she had no way of knowing any of its potential effects, nor did she care. If the laws gave legal immunity, I would find a way for that to change, too.

A few days later, I emailed Attorney Miller, realizing Mr. Rosario's case would not be successful, especially since he had officially resigned. My email included a long investigative list to consider. I guess Attorney Miller figured I had watched too many episodes of Suits because he fiercely dismissed me. He charged me with not trusting him and breaking the attorney-client relationship. After a few more angry expressions, he encouraged me to choose another attorney from the teacher's association.

I responded with a simple I understand, and I apologized. Attorney Miller was correct. I did not trust him. He bailed twice to view the videos, gave me the PIA to skim through with little directions, and asked Mr. Rosario to provide the initial representation agreement form. Attorney Miller gave ample reasons not to trust him. There were no bad feelings, for I figured everything was in Divine order. Whenever I could, I helped Mr. Rosario with his case. I gave Attorney Miller the result of my claim after receiving them from the district's attorney. I did not have the heart to tell Mr. Rosario why I was not with the attorney when he wanted me to return. He did not know Attorney Miller kicked me to the curb; I just took the blame. Besides, the PIA was enough to prove racial disparities, and any decent attorney could see that.

I attempted with another attorney in the teacher's organization as a referral from another law firm. He asked if I wanted to sue the district. When I responded yes, this attorney declined, stating he was not doing that currently. I figured there was no reason to contact another attorney from the teacher's association. I searched for other cases against the district and called those attorneys. However, only one of the two returned the call but worked on behalf of students. I gazed through to the end of the school year. I decided to resume my attorney search during the summer. It would give me more time as well as time to sort my emotions without work distractions.

Summer for educators is a coveted time. After enduring the demanding workload, students, staff, and parents' personalities while balancing home, educators can finally step off the balance beam. I now fixed my focus on addressing the district leaders and finding an attorney if needed. Between planning and organizing our church's Vacation Bible School and researching the laws to resolve my claim, the summer was not relaxing.

Since I planned to seek legal assistance, I requested Attorney Miller notify the district of no longer representing me. It was then I received a response from the chief of leadership officer regarding my letter. The chief leadership officer informed me she would oversee handling my racism charge. When she asked about legal representation for correspondence, I pretended to know what I was doing. She wanted to know if I had an attorney, and it was apparent.

I decided to wait until I had a chance to meet with the district officials before finding another lawyer. My ultimate desire was that God is seen in me and not an angry person seeking revenge. Attempting to punish the entire district and those invested was not the goal. The goal was a change. Change in how leaders treated employees. Change in how children left in the hands of possible abusers because the abuser was a friend of someone in higher positions. Change in racial disparities in hiring practices of minorities. Change so that children and staff of all races were respected and valued.

As I reflected on mine and others' experiences on the middle school campus, I grew more determined for change. The only reason I was able to withstand the disparity of treatment was another Black teacher's testimony and encouragement. Being new to the school and district, I eventually gathered the courage for discussion. Mistreatment causes barriers to form, and you do not know who is trustworthy. In frustration, I confided my desire to leave because of frequent unmerited meetings with the school's administration.

She encouraged, "To leave is what they want you to do. I received the same treatment when I first came here. Admin left me alone when I switched to teaching all regular classes and not honors students."

I could not understand how to deal with this situation. It was my first experience with this level of workplace discomfort. I walked out of each meeting, confused, and second-guessed everything I did. After continuous surveillance and calls to the office, I confided in the same co-worker again.

"I wonder why you? Why are they continuously picking on you?" In her years of being there, even she did not experience that amount of pressure.

I would not suggest only teaching all regular classes since my teaching practices were never a concern previously. Perhaps that was their goal. Later, another Black teacher, new to the campus, suggested more involvement in after school activities to show dedication. With four children, I rightfully dedicated my after-school time and energy to my family. I was not going to neglect my family to get someone to respect and like me. I maintained my commitment during contracted hours. When I needed to catch up on grading papers, lesson plans, or inputting grades, I sacrificed time at home.

Not even a few weeks after the suggestion, she became a target as well. She was energetic, loved the students, and put her time and money into her classroom. Her classroom was the most visually engaging in the building. Her connection with the students was impeccable, often including open mic poetry, rap music, and other strategies to engage students.

Sadly, she realized because of her Blackness, she could not outshine her White counterparts. The district spent tens of thousands of dollars attempting to inspire teachers to incorporate Ron Clark's classroom methods. They could have saved the money and hired her to assist other teachers. Instead, they robbed her joy and energetic drive and sent her into hopelessness.

One morning with the former principal, Paula, Denise, and two other educators perused her classroom like Sherlock Holmes' investigative team. The classroom's cafe-style theme had various tables and a red booth in the center of the room. It was the only classroom in the building with this much charisma and effort to create an environment child loved. I watched from my quaint corner classroom as four White educators condemned her classroom as unsuitable for student learning. A district's specialist from the English department came a little later. She briefly walked into the room, but returned to the hallway, looking at students' work. I was impressed she did not engage in the foolery.

A week later, the teacher rented a U-Haul to remove all the tables, keeping the red booth as permitted. As she loaded her belongings and dismantled her classroom, she also removed herself emotionally. The students were disappointed as much as the teacher. Paula's oppressive ways again were evident with the Black staff.

The teacher transferred after the school year and was eventually promoted to a leadership position. While this was a great victory for her, it was short-lived as she would have to file grievances for the hostile workplace at other campuses within the district. She eventually left. Before leaving, she confided that she wished she had refused to leave the first school under the pressure of a hostile work environment. We realized if you moved, you became the problem regardless of the evidence presented. After my reflections, it was imperative to continue the process with the district leaders.

On June 18, 2019, I received an email from the district's assistant general counsel requesting to meet with me and other school staff. I wondered if she was assigned because she was Black, and I did not have attorney representation. The chief leadership officer who initially stated that she would handle the claim was White. Traumatic events dim perception causing doubt in most similar situations. Regardless of my thoughts, I wanted to discuss the concerns, at least.

After requesting the videos again, the assistant general counsel mailed to the state's attorney general, seeking permission to deny. The denial prompted me to seek assistance from the state's attorney general department to release records. I realized this meeting would not be honest dialogue and accountability. I tested my hypothesis by telling the district's assistant counsel I would not come in for the meeting but would call. She responded that the investigation would continue without my input. It was an option to call in given to several staff members, including me, in her initial email. Her actions confirmed my belief this was a ploy to make me feel heard, but nothing would change. My husband's insight was they wanted to make sure I did not have an attorney. I also sent an email that I had found the law regarding CPS case procedures. She did not reply.

The days before the meeting, I recalled the biography of Queen Esther. Like Esther, I fasted and prayed for guidance and insight. Like Esther, my obedience had to outweigh my fears to make a difference for people subjected to rulers of darkness instead of God's love and acceptance. The chances were slim, but if I could allow God to use me, perhaps those coming behind me would get a better chance at justice.

I went to the district's general counsel's office as planned. Hugging the receptionist, a former co-worker, I did not say anything about my purpose for being there during the summer. I also tried to make sure she did not notice my fear by engaging in a little small talk. I was alone and felt extremely uncomfortable. On the elevator to the third floor, I prayed for the correct words and to not cry. Many restless nights and the overarching burdens left me inept at withstanding the pressures.

The assistant general counsel greeted pleasantly, extending her hand. She led me into a basic, double-entry, rectangular-shaped conference room with an oval table that could seat about twenty or more people. She offered water before taping our conversation. I refused, not wanting any food items or liquids from anyone. She had the letter, flipping through it with her notes in the margin. Appearing attentive, she asked questions and listened and occasionally prompted for clarification of some responses.

I requested water as I attempted to force back the voice shakiness that comes before releasing emotions. Supportively, she went to get it. As she opened the door, making a slight turn to the right, she extended her hand with a smile to get the water bottle. My husband's reminder of others listening to the conversation came to mind. She returned with the bottle of water, and the conversation continued.

She asked about my reasons for the racism claim. I responded. "What else could it be? Let's just say it was favoritism. What is the discriminating factor for the favoritism that allowed a person who was the perpetrator in a CPS case to remain on campus without proper investigation? Why would Bernadine Clark and Janie Lang support both leaders who harassed and retaliated? Again, what is the discriminating factor? Is it color? Age? Gender? Religion? There's a factor in which Brock and Mandy gained an advantage. I believe it's racism."

She nodded as a listening response.

The PIA was not a mystery. What is in black and white usually prevails. Suppose the district's reason for Brock remaining on campus was they did not want the public to know about the principal's CPS report. How could they explain the retaliation? I went on to explain as an adult, I would eventually get over Brock and Mandy's mistreatment. However, the possibility of what was done to the child was not acceptable. I shared with the district's assistant attorney if one of my children were in the same situation, I could only hope someone would fight for mine. She nodded her but never responded to this statement.

The district's assistant attorney also did not ask about the Child Protective Service's report or what the recordings identified. Why not allow me to view the tapes to view Brock's innocence and support why he remained on campus. Why would Brock retaliate for the report? Why did Mandy get involved, and Janie have a concern about Brock's friendship with John Lee?

I followed the letter I wrote as advised by a good friend to stay focused. When I told her Brock's comment to a Black teacher assistant regarding eating monkeys, she raised her eyebrows in disbelief shaking her head. I summed Brock's behavior as being too brazen because of the support from the area director, human resource director, and the district's investigator.

I addressed Mandy's behaviors and comments. I explained how Mandy openly compared our salaries to justify why I needed to take on her responsibilities. I continued from the letter discussing Mandy's degrading remarks about my hairstyle and fake Christians. As I read from the letter and grievances, I could not believe all that occurred.

I questioned why Janie Lang was the only investigator in the district. I asked who reviewed her findings for transparency. The fate of all employees lay within the hands of one person during investigations. We discussed how I never received a final report for either the CPS case or the Tiramisu cake with alcohol from Janie Lang. It was not until I received the PIA when I noticed Janie's findings from the cake incident. The assistant general counsel assured I would get a written statement when the investigation was completed.

She asked about the previous incident at the Blue Valley Middle School, where I was a teacher. I continued my defense on the necessity of changing how the district allowed the mistreatment of Black employees. "How does an area director pat me on the back for having courage and honesty regarding racial concerns, then sum up the meeting with it is, what it is? Then suggest I go to a school which is known to have predominantly Black students and staff."

The former area director who gave me this response probably knew the district was deeply rooted in racial practices and perhaps felt powerless. Her compliments promoted a positive image on my behalf. Still, I was left in an abusive environment to fend for myself. What could have happened if she had reported Paula and advised to file a grievance? Would this step have started the process of change earlier? Paula's behaviors continued with other Black educators. Regardless of my opinions on the former area direction's actions, there was a responsibility to report federal law's infractions.

While in the meeting, I asked to view the videos.

She responded, "Oh, you still want to see the videos? I will see what time we can schedule and let you know."

It never happened. The assistant attorney ignored my email request to view the videos when we discuss her investigative findings. Later, I realized the videos were the legal team's department. There was no reason I could not have viewed them the same day. It was just a reminder that the district would choose to cover up all five perpetrators, empowering them to continue whatever behaviors they decided.

I left the office feeling all eyes were on me. And people were in the background mocking this one Black woman who thought she had the power to fight against an entire district who had a legal team and resources at their fingertips. Though the feelings roared within, so did obedience and total surrender. Throughout time, God used people to accomplish His work. We falsely believe "Be still and know that I am God" means God does all the work. God wants our enemies to withdraw and see that He is God. God works through humanity; through those who allow Him. One of many examples was Mary, the mother of Jesus, who had a challenging assignment. Mary, a teenage mother, accepted God's call when women did not have elaborate baby showers, or pregnancy photoshoots, especially while having a baby out of wedlock. Her relationship with God was full surrender and willingness to be shunned, ridiculed, and possibly abandoned by her fiancé.

Our assignments will not look the same. Joseph's job was to care and support Mary, and later to rear Jesus as his son. Joseph faced the same concerns as Mary. I am sure many assumed he had defiled Mary by having sexual relations before marriage. He endured what her family thought of him and their concerns whether he would keep Mary as his future wife. I am sure his "boys" had many questions and comments.

Together Mary and Joseph risked their reputation and accepted a task that could have caused a strain in their relationship. Joseph married Mary but could not consummate the marriage until after the birth of Jesus and her cleansing period. As he watched his bride's womb expand, he watched knowing their first child was not his blood. The expectation of the Heavenly responsibility no doubt weighed his heart. As with any new mother, I am sure Mary labored over the child-rearing expectations. I cannot imagine the agony.

We will all have a task. Just because we are afraid or have feelings of being ridiculed, our emotions do not give us the right to neglect the assignment. Neglect leads to limiting the spiritual results on Earth as it is in Heaven, thus allowing darkness to rule and hover over our situations and conditions. We cannot rely solely on yesterday's victories of those who came before us. The Spiritual mantle must continue, for the need to exercise faith is in high demand. Change occurs when each person decides to allow God's will to flow through them.

When the call is from God, we can expect valleys. However, we know the Shepherd leads, and His rod and staff will protect and comfort as we travel through the valleys. The Good Shepherd will guide us to a resting place within Him, like green Pasteur, which nourishes our souls. We do not have to fear evil because He is with us.

Chapter 16

Tug of War

The district's assistant attorney kept her word of having a written report. I was at Wednesday night's bible study preparing for the youth when I noticed the email the investigation was complete. The results would come after the district-wide summer break. I knew if anyone waited two weeks to give you the results, it was not good. What for what? Why not wait until you were able to provide me with the conclusive findings?

I filed a complaint with the Attorney General's office regarding the district's refusal to release the videos. After a friend informed me that I could file a complaint about educator misconduct, I sought assistance from the Texas Education Agency. I contacted numerous attorneys, including a college friend's dad. His daughter and I had a mutual friend, but neither of us knew how to reach her. Her father was excellent in his field and assisted me before in legal matters. He would guide me or take the case.

With one of the attorney's recommendations to follow the process of communicating with the district and then contact the United States Equal Employment Opportunity Commission (EEOC), I completed the online form. Though, there was no availability for an in-person interview. I was reluctant if a date would come available. June filled my days with plenty of unknowns, doubt, and prayer to release my concerns in God's hand. It was appropriate to practice stillness before God for the time to do anything else had not come.

In July, I went on a scheduled girl's trip, "sister cuzs," as my sisters and cousins called it. Since we missed our first cousin's inauguration as president of Lincoln University, we decided to visit her in Jefferson City, Missouri. Traveling with one of my sisters, we stopped in Tulsa, Oklahoma, to slow down the trip and enjoy the visit. My sister was gracious to entertain my regurgitation of everything I was going through. Several times, I attempted to stop talking. I wanted to stop; I needed to stop talking about it. I knew this was supposed to be a relaxing trip, free of life's regular drama. Only at various moments did the conversation drift to different subjects.

We arrived at the hotel and decided to eat at the restaurant within walking distance of the hotel. It was a barbeque place that was not barbeque, at least not what we were desiring. It did not meet the standards of women traveling. Good food is a requirement on any vacation.

The battle between being fully present and removed from the district's last response divided my thoughts. My mind desperately tried to be fully present and connect. Although I was with good company, I was lonely. Space and time elude the present when circumstances are not favorable. You drift, hoping to land in the right place at the right moment, and with the desired results.

I could not reconcile my feelings for leaders who decided integrity was an option. How anyone sees the evidence, the videos, and simply disregard another human being, one being a child, was beyond my comprehension. However, through my Christian responsibility, I prayed for them. I recalled my grandfather's words as my mother taught, "People don't understand." It was not until I became more life experienced that I understood. People do not know how the consequences of behaviors will outweigh the snippet of enjoyment.

The way we live our lives is a daily offering to God. God can and will choose to either accept or refuse the offering. When Cain became angry when God rejected his offering, God responded to Cain by asking questions first, prompting Cain's responses. Then He told Cain, "And if you do well, will you not be accepted? And if you do not do well, sin lies at the door. And its desire is for you, but you should rule over it" (Genesis 4:7). The problem with choosing the wrong paths intentionally is you allow sin to rule. Sin waits for us to disobey. Once sin leads, we become a vessel for evil, used by our real enemy, Satan. People do not understand the enormous spiritual impact their choices have on them, their families, and those in their care. As Satan rules, you do not turn off his control by location. Every place you step, whether home, work, friendships, church, etc., you give Satan access if you choose to sin. Sin is not selective; it wants all.

Brock's and Mandy's behavior potentially impacted a child for a lifetime, and through this child lineage and familial ties. Their choices flowed over into the school's environment, students, and parents. The new principals would endure the uncertain environment, and eventually Brock and Mandy's families when they discovered their real character. Their behavior also impacted the district leaders. District leaders, standing at accountability's crossroad, decided which road to travel. Wrong decisions at critical moments often surface. If the ability to take a more in-depth look, we would discover the depths of Brock's choice impacted the entire district.

One person's sin impacted an entire nation, Israel, in Joshua, chapter 7. Because Achan decided to steal items from the Babylonians, which God had instructed against, Israel lost the war with Ai, a small group of people. Achan admitted he coveted first. Often, we want what God despises, such as power, fame, control, or wrongfully gained wealth. God could have called out the sin before the battle; however, most lessons are more impactful when we learn them because of our actions.

We pray for our enemies because their choices impact more people than we could imagine, sometimes extending into generations. To stop the cycle of abuse when sin rules, we must learn to pray for our enemies' souls. We pray for God to intervene and change their hearts towards Him. Many times, the words of my prayers did not match my feelings. However, we must want what God desires. If we get caught up in our feelings, then we are not able to do Kingdom work. Praying for opposing people brings us closer to God. Our faith to pray indicate we trust God to do what is necessary and best.

Praying for your enemies takes effort and honesty. It is not God's desire to ignore the emotions He created in us. It is God who said to be angry but do not sin (Ephesians 4:26). It is healthy to explore and to accept the feelings. Our emotions assist healing in various ways. However, God desires we rule over our emotions after working through them. I was angry at Brock and Mandy many days, but I did not choose to retaliate in anger. However, I did have the righteous choice to seek justice. It is not retaliatory behavior when we use the law or spiritual principles to protect ourselves.

I prayed for those directly responsible for neglecting the child's and my rights. I also prayed for those who now had the arduous task of making sure justice prevailed. There are many puzzle pieces in an organization. Most often, an organization will make decisions to abort public scrutiny. It is understandable as most people operate in ways that give others the best impression of themselves. We want others to trust and believe in us, so we make decisions to cover up the truth. For the situation to become public knowledge that a counselor reported a principal for indecency with a child and those five involved allowed the principal to stay on campus without a formal investigation, it would cause an uproar among the parents. To deny parents the right to know was an injustice.

However, understanding a position does not justify the choice. We often fail to realize darkness will not hide forever. Although God gives grace, grace is for repentance, not to continue sinning. Protecting darkness or sin is sinful. God is not a man that He should lie, so when he states, "For nothing is secret that will not be revealed, nor anything hidden that will not be known and come to light," we can trust it. (Luke 8:17 NKJV). It does not necessarily mean the grape you ate in the store, though it may. The replication of sin hinders us from becoming more Christ-like.

I also prayed for someone to have the courage to trust God's word. God has His people in the right places and positions, but the people must choose to serve Him in those places and situations. Surely, there would be one who would take the baton from me and finish the race. With the video recordings and the trail of emails as evidence, how difficult could it be to influence others to stand on the side of justice? During the wait time of the results, my constant prayer was, "God, let there be at least one."

Eventually, I was able to be present on the sister cuz girl's trip. I forced it as I did not want to ruin the trip by constantly retelling the details. It was not fair to any of us. My cousin was a very gracious host, and as most women do when we get together, we chatted and laughed until the early morning hours. I was more relaxed on the road trip home but wondered what the results would be and how fair the district officials would rule.

July 17, 2019, I received the investigation results without an invitation to discuss or view the videotapes. The letter opened with my claim of being subjected to race discrimination and harassment, producing a hostile work environment by the five named district employees. The second paragraph discussed the investigation included sixteen individuals interviewed. The big reveal stated that I had presented "sufficient evidence" to support my above allegations against Brock, and insufficient evidence for the others based on the information obtained. There was not one word or letter regarding CPS or videos.

A few of the interviewed people discussed the questions asked were about the school's environment and Brock. It was ludicrous for district leaders to expect others to know Brock's and Mandy's actions towards me or feel comfortable enough to say. Furthermore, those interviewed were not privy to the actions of the elementary area director, the human resource director, nor the district's investigator. To say I was disappointed is, to say the very least. Although I do not know the investigation protocols, a simple conversation would have stopped my efforts. Acknowledging racism, workplace harassment, and a hostile work environment in a letter without resolution adds to the abuse.

Interestingly, I received a CPS call regarding a complaint against Brock the same day I received the results. When I asked the CPS caseworker the child's name, she stated that she did not have any other details other than the child's age. I would not give her any concerns about Brock since she was withholding information. How could I give her information about a random child according to age? The school had at least forty children at the age she gave me. She said she would gather more information and call me back. I called her the following week and left a message, but I never heard from her again.

I wanted to scream. I screamed. How could people deny the recorded and written truth? I could not fathom the idea that no one, not one of the leaders, cared enough to speak out. Not one person attempted to have a conversation with me, just addressed me with merely a little over a page letter. An entire leadership team revealed you are not important without a lawyer. I now understood why Brock's confidence and pride beamed. He knew the system would protect him. The district's message rang clearly; abuse, and racism are acceptable.

To ease my mind, I scanned Facebook for anything comical or encouraging. I came across a video from Judge Lynn talking about her mother's wisdom. She shared her mother's words, "It's not time to fall apart. Now is the time to hold it together." This encouragement pulled me from a defeatist attitude to asking God, "What's next?"

Chapter 17

Faith Tested

Understanding some answers come by prayer and fasting, I committed to doing so before taking the next step of filing with the U. S. Equal Employment Opportunity Commission. During that time, I received a letter from the Texas Attorney General's office requiring the school district to release the public information I requested, including the videos. The district did not meet the 10-day deadline, so the recordings should be released as required by law. However, the Attorney General's office gave an extension to submit their reasons for not issuing the request. When the Attorney General granted the right to withhold based on the Family Education Rights and Privacy Acts, I discontinued fighting to get the videos. After all, they had attorneys. I could not secure an attorney to review my information. The one attorney, who I was positive would help, I could not connect with him.

July was the longest of my summer months as I waited to hear from T.E.A. and E.E.O.C. I checked the E.E.O.C. website almost daily. The calendar on their website did not have any available dates to schedule. It was my litmus test. If a time came available, then I would continue the process. If not, I would drop it.

With the time to mentally process information, I realized the weight of it all. I decided to return to the counselor I had met to help with the stress. She was recommended by a friend who had also experienced workplace harassment in the same district. My first visit with her left me feeling peculiar, so I had not scheduled the remaining four appointments left provided by the district's employee assistance program. She was no-nonsense, direct, and not an emotional rescuer, which was not what I wanted. I wanted someone to feel sorry for me and angry with the district.

My first visit, I went in with whatever wrinkled gym clothing, no makeup, and hair pulled up in a wide colorful headband but no extra attempts to make it look nice. I did not want to be strong or appear secure as I had been to so many people. I wanted to be the one who received a shoulder to cry. I saw the Bible on one of her side tables in the unassuming office; I felt I was in the right place to wallow in my sorrows. Pausing between tears, I told her the events, starting with the C.P.S. case and ending with the retaliation. She looked annoyed. I continued to talk, seeking whatever emotion she was willing to give. However, she did just the opposite.

In her Ghanaian accent, she sighed and said, "You love details. I'm going to teach you how to have thick skin." I could not believe I poured out an expanded version of details, and she could not even get angry at the apparent racism. Here was a Black woman from the heart of the Motherland, and she wanted to focus on the toughness of my skin. My skin did not want to be tough anymore. It had enough. After the scheduled hour, I left and called my sister once I got in my car. I laughed so uncontrollably I could barely get the words out that this was my first counseling session. In between laughs, I told her what the counselor stated.

Realizing God was not about to allow me to pretend He had not prepared me for this moment and purpose, my heart changed its course. I wrote in my journal about faith. *Help me, Lord, to have faith that everything is working out for my good. Faith is when I can trust you even when I do not see a "winning" outcome. Faith is when I believe you are in the background cooking up the best food to prepare my table before my enemies. Faith is letting go to move forward.*

Faith is returning to the very place that wrecked my spirit with my head up high because I am learning to walk in your precepts, and no shame comes from that. Faith is singing praises to Your Name in my distress, knowing you are my salvation. Faith is continuing to march on as spiritual men and women marched in Your Name, believing Your promises are true and fulfilled. Faith is saying, "Though He slays me, yet I will trust Him." Faith is saying though I walk through the valley of death, I will fear no evil for Thou art with me. Faith says this mountain, too, will be moved. Faith says, watch my God!

Faith is not as "earthly" wins; these things will wipe away and only benefit you or your immediate circle. Faith without the appearance of winning is Kingdom winning. Spiritual fortitude where God sees He can trust you with anything! Faith is eating an apple instead of the pound cake, knowing the weight will not come off immediately. If you eat the apples instead of the pound cake, the weight will come off as it is with spiritual weight. The more we walk in faith, the more we can remove what spiritually kills us. Jesus said, take my yoke. My yoke is easy. Without faith, we cannot understand or believe in this principle.

Faith gave me the courage to return to the same campus. I made a good on "I'm not running" stance. The new school year started with two different administrators from another campus. As counselors talked among one another, I knew principals did as well. I was very apprehensive about the relationships. The constant worry of how much they knew, what Mandy had untruthfully shared, and the fact Sally returned was enough to make me quit. More than likely, Sally remained in constant contact with Brock and Mandy. However, leaving was not an option, especially after you take a stand.

The Texas Education Agency (T.E.A.) responded to my allegations. I opened the email at work. With anxiety looming, it appeared there was not a resolution. I was very disappointed and fearful the district would learn of my complaint to T.E.A. and retaliate. The entire afternoon, I contemplated how T.E.A. did not see the evidence. Apparently, the agency upheld the wrongdoings Brock and Mandy and other district leaders.

After arriving home, my intuition led me to reread the letter. The letter divided my complaint into four areas and addressed each area with directions on proceeding legally. My claim, transferred to the State Board for Educator Certification (S.B.E.C.), a department within T.E.A., for further review was the next phase. I realized the anxiety of receiving the response caused me not to understand what I read earlier. From that point on, I made sure to take daily walks after work to help my mind and body relax.

As advised from the letter, I completed complaints to the Office of Civil Rights in Dallas, Texas, and the Texas Workforce Commission. I spoke with the O.C.R. regarding the child as well. It was confusing when they asked if I wanted to file a complaint on the child's behalf. I was unsure of the process, so I felt this was not the correct path. Without any district documentation as to what evidence was factual and specific allegations for Brock, I felt this was not the correct path. Both entities advised me to continue the E.E.O.C. process since I had a complaint on file.

October 2, 2019, a final status letter from S.B.E.C. arrived in my email. Another one-page message stated, "This letter is to notify you that, after considering all information gathered during our review, the division will not be opening an investigation. Therefore, Educator Investigations has closed the complaint." There were no specifics and no interviews or phone calls with me. However, it was not unexpected. I wrote in my journal on September 21, 2019, "I haven't heard from S.B.E.C. The last time I saw *the area director, she appeared to be more relaxed than previously, leading me to believe she knows she's in the clear."*

I took the second paragraph as a warning not to waste my time asking for a report. The first sentence stated, "Please be aware that T.E.A. follows the Texas Public Information Act to release information." It was the same maneuver used to deny viewing the videos. I figured that without an attorney, it was a waste of time to refute.

My last and final dance with the district had to be with E.E.O.C. and securing a lawyer. E.E.O.C.'s calendar opened for October 17, 2019. A friend advised me to make a binder so that the interviewer could easily view an organized timeline. I spent many nights after work printing and assembling the binder with a table of contents. Papers sometimes printed as duplicates as I tried to keep up with it all. My daughter's twin bed held each stack. I attempted to show the district's inner workings in an easily readable fashion. When I got off tracked with the table of contents and the paperwork's order, I used a red pen to correct it. I was too exhausted to fix the errors. After work and often, after taking care of my family, the work's intensity became grueling.

On October 17, I took off a half-day of work, came home to pray. I ate a half sandwich, grabbed the binder in my work bag, and headed downtown Dallas. Maneuvering through downtown Dallas, I found parking and went into the building that housed the E.E.O.C. office.

After going through the security check, I located the office. It was quiet, with only two mid-twenties ladies chatting behind me. I was stunned. For the calendar to have no openings, I assumed it would have as many people as the Department of Public Safety. I checked in, sat down, and waited. I prepared by bringing a book to read before for the interview. Two additional men came in. When asked to go to the back, one of the men remained in the lobby as he was not allowed to accompany his brother.

A young Black lady opened the door and called for me. The office was small, with only the basics of an office. It appeared to be perhaps a shared workspace or a newly appointed to the position. She seemed to be attentive and took many notes. However, she stated that my claim was not pervasive enough for their agency to take the case. The example she gave was if someone left a noose on my desk, that would be a case their office would consider. For some reason, the E.E.O.C. interviewer did not look through my prepared binder of emails, the PIA, and letters from various agencies even though I offered. She went to get advice from her supervisor on whether a right to sue could be issued.

As I waited, my prayer was for God's will. If the answer was no, then this was the end of the road. A part of me hoped she returned with her supervisor, rejecting my claim so that I could have a valid reason to quit. She returned with explaining the process, the district's notification, and the ninety day window to file the complaint. Before leaving, she gave a list of attorneys to call. I was satisfied I accomplished this much. I was excited to tell those who knew I had the letter to proceed forward. It felt odd to sue a company while working for it. I had no idea how difficult it would be to get an attorney to listen to the case much more to review the information.

I did not have success with finding a lawyer who was willing to meet on contingency. I understood everyone has a bill to pay, so I was ready to pay for a case review. After researching, emailing, and calling several lawyers, I finally decided on a firm. Again, I had my overload of unneeded paperwork.

The lawyer assigned to meet with me was young, and two years out of law school, I later learned. He jotted notes as I talked, but not particularly interested in the paperwork I brought with me. He steamrolled when mentioning his retainer and hourly fees. Then he ran down the possible amount to sue and told me I had to quit my job to file the lawsuit more than likely. According to him, most companies offered a payout with the agreement to separate.

There were two significant problems with the meeting. One, I did not have the money upfront to hand over for possibilities and future billables. With two college-age children and one in elementary, it was necessary I at least believed he could handle the case successfully. We talked more about church than the case, so I did not see this as a certainty. Perhaps he was spending time to justify my one hundred and fifty dollars meeting that technically ended in ten minutes. Secondly, he spoke too fast about the money, a warning sign. My oldest sister taught me when someone talks too quickly intentionally, it is a trap, so walk away. He offered to take the case, but I left a little discouraged, seeing all the odds stacked against me.

A few weeks later, I finally contacted my college friend, Esther, whose dad was the attorney I could not make contact during the summer. It was immediate relief. I knew he was well versed in school law as well as civil rights. He would stand firm as well as make sure equity prevailed. With his background and knowledge, I believed my chances went from zero to a thousand. After weeks receiving rejected case letters, a few return phone calls, and having lawyers advising to leave the district, I could breathe.

Esther sent my phone number as well as called her father. He contacted me on the same day. On a Wednesday evening, he left a message on my cell phone to send the E.E.O.C. a right to sue letter and a detailed narrative. I called both his work and cell numbers to get a better understanding of the narrative. When he did not answer either, I sent over the letter I wrote to the district. Knowing he was currently in a court case, I decided to wait a week to give him a chance to review my paperwork.

Five days later, I received a text from a mutual college friend, asking if I saw Esther's Facebook posts. I was sitting in the assistant principal's office when the next text came through and sent shock waves through me. It was Esther's lovely tribute to her father. Attorney John W. Walker died.

For five days, I felt a sense of relief and confidence after contacting him. John W. Walker was a well-known civil rights attorney in Little Rock, Arkansas, and a member of the Arkansas House of Representatives. He had the experience, the heart, and my trust. Esther, and I were college friends. I became acquainted with some of the family as we made quick road trips from the University of Arkansas in Pine Bluff to their Little Rock's family residence.

Suddenly oxygen left the room. My hands shook while the rest of my body went numb as I tried to make sense if this was reality. My face felt hot, and I began to sweat. To get out of the building quickly, I asked the assistant principal if she wanted anything from Starbucks. Briskly walking down the hallway, I texted my friend to please be available so that I could talk in a couple of minutes. My thoughts flooded me with each step I took. *How could this possibly be true? How was Esther? Was he sick? Are you kidding me, God? What will I do now? Should I text Esther? Is it too soon?*

Once in the car, I called my friend, "Girl, what in the world?"

"I know, right?" she chuckled in disbelief.

She knew of the many months and times we both tried to locate Esther. The quick conversation was more of repeated questions of how this could happen. I bought unwanted coffee from Starbucks as evidence I did go where I said I would. Returning to my office, I sat at my desk. The weight of the case returned heavier than previously. I did not know what to think or what to do next. The coffee cup and I stared at each other.

I reflected on the day after Attorney Walker called. I told my husband no one could handle the case if he could not resolve it. I would leave it alone if he advised me to do so. Now, I stood alone in a pool of hopelessness and despair. I wanted so desperately for someone to rescue me and get me out of the mess.

Several questions bombarded my mind. How do you move in God when you feel as though even God has deserted you? Why didn't God allow me to connect with Attorney Walker during the summer when God knew he had more time to help? Perhaps I saw notoriety in an attorney than faith in God. Was this the lesson to trust God in complete isolation? I felt selfish for having these thoughts as a good friend no longer had her father, her best friend.

It took two weeks even to consider whether to continue trying. Leaning towards leaving it alone, two ladies within two days encouraged me. Both were Black women working in the district. She recently left a more diverse district where her skin color did not indicate her intelligence and professionalism. The other spoke of the spiritual ramification and God's purpose for me. Believing I had the necessary evidence to make a difference, they incited me to look at the history of those who struggled more than I ever would. I decided to continue until the 90-day mark, giving it my all. Even if there were no visible results, I could be at peace with God and myself.

For encouragement, I reminded myself of a Women's Day breakfast, where I spoke on the title, "Hands-off is Going to Cost You." Hands-off or not moving in the light of God has cost many of us our marriages, our children, our churches, our friendships, our constitutional rights, and freedoms. We must understand this is God's work.

If we continue to take the approach that I will pray for you, but I will not step up to assist where needed, our prayers are in vain. Faith without works is dead. We must not separate Christianity from our daily living. Admittedly, not every battle is ours to take on, but not every battle is ours to overlook.

I did not ask God to allow me to see Brock's behavior with the child. I could have overlooked it. I could have taken the option of not reporting for the safety of my concerns, such as working relationships, proper evaluation, and not having to deal with retaliation for making a C.P.S. report. I did not ask God to allow me to know about Mr. Rosario's previous story. I did not go searching for information to start a fight. I learned through prayer that in this battle, God called me as the vessel for His work.

We are all called to be instruments of God according to His purposes. We must remember it is His choice and not ours. With a set of gifts, skills, and talents, we can accept any legal career path by God's grace. Our willingness to allow God's work to flow through us in our chosen careers increases our value on Earth and Heaven. Matthew 5:14-16 gives insight into the importance of an obedient Christian, "You are the world's light-a city on a hill, glowing in the night for all to see. Do not hide the light. Let it shine for all; let your good deeds glow for all to see so that they will praise your Heavenly Father."

Chapter 18

Not About You

Mandy's words resonated in my mind, "It's not about you." Though I knew this, my focus became about my life and feelings as I felt defeated, trying to help the child and Mr. Rosario. Writing my story during the significant events, the deaths of George Floyd and BreonnaTaylor, and the COVID-19 virus, I watched as opposing sides argued their opinions. Many believed the protests were not valid or not warranted as the world shook and rocked demanding justice.

Having to accept the outcomes, I concluded to share my story so that others could hopefully see the truth. The truth is the laws in the wrong hands do not work. The truth that nonviolent protests are sometimes needed.

It is also true we understand that racism is not just a problem for people of color. Racism impacts the very existence of who we are. Racism divides homes, workplaces, churches, and every part of society. A house divided will not stand. Once we allow division, we fall. When we fall, skin color or political agendas will not sustain us. If someone is drowning, I doubt the person chooses death over the extended hand regardless of skin color or political agenda.

Racism, harassment, and discrimination should not ever be the norm. We are responsible for the care of one another. God will not ask us how often we washed our cars, how clean we kept our homes, or how many awards we received from our careers. The question we will all have to answer is, how did you love? Love does not walk away or turn the eye to injustices.

My soul labored reliving painful moments, as I wrote. Some days, I saw things I did not see while going through the trials. I figured if I decided not to publish then at the very least, I released my emotions through the process of my narrative. I believed writing was my new assignment, so I pushed to obedience. I pushed through doubt anyone would read it or want to read the story. I pushed through the thinking my family and friends thought that I had finally lost it due to the traumatic events of trying to fight a giant. I only broke away from writing when it was too much to experience the world in turmoil intertwined with personal pain.

As I was about to wrap up my story, I prayed, asking God, how do you want me to end this? I knew I could complete it my way, but something felt incomplete. I settled in my heart I was obedient to the call, and in due season God will deal with those who chose to be carriers of darkness instead of light. Though it may not look like success to some, it was a success for me. I stayed the course. I fought the fight and gave everything I had within me.

As my spiritual strengthening, I listened daily to sermons. Recently listening to Dr. Charles Stanley's sermon about creating a space specifically for prayer, I retreated to my closet. I prayed before writing as it was as much God's story as it was mine. I did not want to hurt those who hurt me in my writing. Well, I did, but I knew God's purpose for everyone is they come into the knowledge of His saving grace. I wanted to be authentic to the narrative and my personality, so I requested guidance with every written word.

I put one of my daughters' discarded tan and silver throw pillow on top of the off-white, hard plastic step stool for comfort. As usual, when I kneel, I saw how I needed to vacuum.

Reminding myself to focus on my purpose, I talked to God. *Father, I feel the task is complete. I know how to end this story spiritually, but I want Your guidance. There will be many who believed it was not worth the trouble I went through. I understand following You is more important than appearances. Tell me how You want this story to end.*

As I stood up, I felt spiritually compelled to call Child Protective Services to inquire if the investigator knew about Brock and the child's videos. I knew if the district officials blocked me from viewing the tapes to the extent of writing to the Attorney General. More than likely, the CPS investigator was unaware. In all the emotional turmoil and searching for an attorney, I did not think to call back after the district denied access to the videos. Inadvertently, my focus shifted to myself since I did not have a recourse to help the child or myself without an attorney. I did not feel going to the parents was an option, especially since Brock friended them.

God reminded me that the entire incident was not about me. Mandy's words were spoken in spiritual truth, though she had no implications of her words. Yes, what Mandy and Brock did, and their leaders allowed were evil. However, their actions excavated the spiritual gifts within me. The events drew me closer to understanding how God uses those He loves for the purposes He chooses. Through the struggles, God allowed the development of my character and grit of my spirit.

My spirit knew God gave direction in my prayer closet. I needed to return to help the child and others by ensuring the truth of light overcame the darkness. However, I began to question His guidance because it was almost two years from the first report. Yes, I tried to get an attorney and told the E.E.O.C. investigator about the child. If the child indeed were violated, therapy would be needed, and the parents needed the tools to help her through the trauma.

Those who protected Brock and Mandy were as dangerous to children as Brock and Mandy. I feared the image of being a crazy, outrageous, and vindictive person. I asked a few friends if they knew of any CPS workers to get guidance before making a complete fool of myself. As advised, I called the caseworker after locating the letter dated December 18, 2018.

I pushed through the insecurities. I chose to sacrifice my reputation believing 1 Samuel 15:22-23, "So Samuel said to Saul, Has the Lord as great delight in burnt offerings and sacrifices, as in obeying the voice of the Lord? Behold, to obey is better than sacrifice, and to heed than the fat of rams. For rebellion is as the sin of witchcraft." My mind recalled the voice of Pricilla Shirer, saying, "Behold! Friends, when we see the word behold, we must understand something great and necessary is coming behind it."

The caseworker could not find the file but told me she remembered me, which made me more insecure as I wondered how she remembered me. Did she recall the little girl perpetrating as a confident counselor who whispered in a closed office? What level of craziness did she rate me on the "girl let me tell you scale" to her coworkers? The CPS caseworker did not know of nor had she seen any videos. She told me to call the main number and make another report to give the new information. I hesitated again, believing someone else will know of my craziness.

Nevertheless, I called the main number expecting to have a long wait as in previous experiences. After listening to the automatic prompts, I immediately connected to an intake operator. Hoping to have wait time music, I had no time to process whether I should report or bow out.

I gave all the information before asking her to make sure she put the previous case number in the notes when she could not find it. At least three times, I reminded her the school district had videos of the incident and blocked me from viewing them. I also realized I was in the habit of giving pronouns without names as she repeatedly asked questions to clarify the pronouns. Perhaps this was the reason things were misunderstood in its entirety the first time I called CPS.

A couple of hours later, a CPS investigator contacted me, the same person who called the previous summer inquiring about Brock without the child's information. Because she did not have the child's name, I thought it was a scam underlined by the district. For some reason, the CPS investigator and I did not connect anymore, but I recalled her name. I reminded her that I left a message during the past summer.

"Why now?" she asked.

I responded, "I know it's the right thing to do morally." I also told her the initial investigator did not view the tapes. I did not think to share the information after realizing how many of them worked together to shield the truth. It was not until May 2019 I received the documents and alerted the district superintendent and a couple of his leadership team. At this point, I was fighting a new battle and trying to find an attorney.

She shared a new investigation would not occur more than likely, but perhaps filed with the local police department. Suddenly, I interrupted whatever she was trying to say. Maybe with age and hormones brought tears or the weight of life just comes in unannounced. Whatever the underlying reason, I pushed through a crackling voice to let this lady know why I called. Stammering the letter L about ten times, trying to speak before she hung up, I shared, "Let me explain. For two years, I have been trying to resolve this. They (district personnel) told us to train people on reporting, and how we can lose our license if we do not. Then I do it and learn no one even cared. No one tried to do anything."

Empathetically she stated, "I understand. You did the right thing to call back. As I said, we probably will not open an investigation again. But it may be something the police department will look into."

I heard the CPS investigator repeating some of her words, but I finally listened to the words "police department." Now I had a new level of personal concern. I was also dealing with college graduation, surviving a pandemic with children, a husband recovering from a blood clot that almost killed him, and now police involvement. I did not need anything else. I did not know if I would be asked questions or must send a written report.

Also, my concerns included not having seen the video. I knew what I saw and felt at that moment, but I wondered if I saw accurately enough. After a friend reminded me not to overthink it, I made a mental list of all that had occurred after I formally completed a grievance to calm my nerves. These things got me through the remainder of the day.

However, when night fell, and I laid down to rest, my mind became an outdoor makeshift drive-in movie theater. In tonight's episode, the top news story was Darline, the school counselor, arrested for false reporting. Since the arrest was quick, she could not retrieve her documents to prove the videos existed. Handcuffed and led out the front door, Darline tried to tell her distraught daughter to post her letter to the superintendent on Facebook to let everyone know the truth.

The school district had an inside detective to say no videos existed and Darline was seeking revenge on Brock and Mandy for believing alcohol was in her cake. However, Mandy was innocent because she was not aware of the alcohol as the business establishment was not required legally to label cakes containing alcohol. The world consoled Mandy with balloons and handmade posters and cards. Mandy spent her time, energy, and money on the ungrateful counselor.

When Darline did not like the investigation results, she claimed racism on the district's upper management simply because they were White. Darline became furious when four of the accused received promotions despite her claim. She decided to write a book about her experience and get the police involved in her scheme by calling CPS. Here we had another Black person playing the race card on hardworking and caring people.

Lights revolving around my bedroom interrupted the movie. A couple of cars passed through the neighborhood around one o'clock in the morning. I knew my thoughts were foolish but waited for the breaking sound of my front door. *The movie resumed with Darline plastered over the news as someone impacted by the recent historical pandemic events. But breaking the law was not going to be tolerated, so it was jail time and a hefty fine to pay. The Left and the Right political parties battled on Twitter. Don Lemon, a CNN commentator, called the President's tweet callous and unjustifiably ridiculous while taking a swig of alcohol. As a Black man in America, he had enough. He was going to drink whenever and wherever he pleased.*

I had enough of tossing and turning and waiting for the imaginary police, so I prayed. "Now, Father, you have given me a creative mind. Thank you for this, but please, in the name of your sweet son, Jesus, cut it off. I need to sleep."

The following day, I saw the CPS investigator's email informing the case's referral to the Child Advocacy Center and the local police department. I researched the web, trying to figure out precisely what the local police department involvement played. It was also shocking to think the case was forwarded quickly based on my conversation with the CPS investigator.

Questions plagued my mind. Did Brock have other pending information in a file with Child Protective Services? Would those who allowed him to remain on campus, talk with the parents, and eventually retaliate against me without consequences, become a part of the investigation? What about the State Board of Education Certification investigation, which I believed was also a sham? How far up the ladder did this entire thing go? Why would anyone allow the possibility of child endangerment in a school to exist? Was this bigger than what I realized?

To get my mind to focus on more pleasurable things, I turned once again to music, recorded sermons, and prayer. Music was my saving grace during this entire ordeal. Tasha Cobb, Le'Andria Johnson, Jonathan Reynolds, and the triumphant voice of Kierra Sheard were a few regular artists I relied on to reduce the feelings of inadequacy and fear. As a reminder of why I was doing any of this, I listened to Anita Wilson's "Perfect Love Song" and "Jesus Will" as well as "My Redeemer Lives" by Nicole Miller. For my praise party and to uplift my spirit, I allowed the upbeat, spiritual force lyrics of Ricky Dillard and many others.

When I needed a spiritual word to continue the spiritual fight, I listened to T.D. Jakes. I found Tony Evans sermons when I needed to love despite the recent interactions of those against me. To increase my determination, I searched for Stephanie Ike's sermons. Although I was busy teaching the children on Wednesday nights, my husband's sermons on Sundays saved and spiritually rooted me weekly. Taking God's word and explaining it in practical ways for living and encouragement is his gifting.

Although my family and friends surrounded me, I trudged this mountain alone with God. One of the many days of feeling isolated, I came across in Genesis, chapter 24. Abraham commissioned his servant to find a wife for his son Isaac. With prayer as his guide, the servant finds Rebekah. In Rebekah's family home, he asked Rebekah's family, Laban's, and Bethuel's opinions regarding Isaac's future marriage. The response led to an understanding that God will allow us to be put into situations alone with Him. They responded, "This thing comes from the Lord; we cannot speak to you either bad or good."

The passage helped me to release friends and family members from the obligation of understanding. I desperately wanted others to feel what I was feeling and frequent encouragement. When something is from the Lord for you, God wants you to surrender to Him fully. Surrender your fears, doubts, concerns, and need for validation. Seeking God through prayer becomes oxygen in lonely times.

Unfortunately, the relationship with God thru prayer is reduced to the magic wishes to have what we desire. Prayer is engaging in a huddle around the throne of God, waiting for the play. Once you receive the call, then action must be done. No one huddles up in any sport around a coach, gets the instructions, but remains around the coach. If the team does not put the play into action, it gambles the game because the instructions stayed with the coach. We must move the faith ball.

Prayer is a purposeful dual relationship. Prayer must be more than "Name it and claim it" for selfish motives only. Abraham's servant did not just call out some random name for Isaac's wife. He did not just stay at Abraham's feet, "naming it and claiming it." The servant received his instructions from Abraham. They consulted regarding the expectations and the rules. Then the servant took those orders, and he "went." The servant realized that he needed assistance, so he prayed to the God of Abraham. He watched God bless Abraham and saw Abraham blessed God by the way Abraham lived his life. The servant and God came into an agreement, and behold, Rebekah came on the scene. Also, the servant is not empty-handed. He prepared to bring what was customary during those days to claim a wife. He did not just show up demanding she followed him to an unknown country and people. There was respect for the task.

We cannot possibly give God enough materially, for He owns it all. However, we can prepare our hearts to receive what God desires from our lives. Like Rebekah and Abraham's servant, we can be willing to leave the safety of certainty to put faith in the action of uncertainty. Remember that what happens to us can conform us to Christ if we allow it. Most often, what God allows is not entirely about us.

Chapter 19

Malignant

Opening my eyes to focus after a long night of sinus pain, I reached and grabbed my phone from the nightstand. The message notifications flashed blue. I read the word 'image' in a new text. It was a picture of the area director, Bernadine Clark, welcoming her to another area school district- a promotion. Her leverage to impact people's lives and students was now a more considerable influence in her new role. Before leaving Lowland ISD, Bernadine Clark received another position that appeared to be a promotion. Two promotions after the allegations.

A person who allowed a principal to remain on a campus with defenseless children can now spread more poison. In an email response to Janie Lang, Bernadine echoed Brock's comment that the parents were angry with the person who made the report. The parents were in good standing with the perpetrator. Bernadine's perspective presumed Brock's innocence without once attempting to speak with me. Of course, I was the monster as claimed by Brock. A monster who risked her welfare and licenses for some unknown reasons.

It was unbelievable someone in her position refused to consider the possibilities of what might have occurred. I could only hope her heart might have changed; however, pride usually seeps in when careless people progress. They continue in selfish ways.

When people who intend to do right by others keep quiet about those who do not, it leaves many in vulnerable positions. We must recognize those who reject God's principles usually bond together. They pull each other up, creating a strong network of people willing to allow anything to succeed. We either choose to live by Godly principles or evil motivations. There is no middle ground. Evil and goodness need hosts; we are the hosts. Since I had the emails, I knew Bernadine made intentional and law-breaking choices and supported Brock's actions. Now, more people than she had in Lowland ISD lie in her hands.

We either allow God to use us, or we do not. There is no in-between. In all moments, especially pivotal moments, we must be hosts for spiritual manifestations. In 1 Samuel chapters 25-27, we have a great example of a woman who allowed God's spirit to reign in her life. It is one of my favorite biblical narratives of a woman named Abigail. Abigail is referred to as beautiful and as a woman with "good understanding." Abigail is the epitome of a Proverbs 31-woman, Allela Keys' Superwoman", and Deborah Cox's "How Did You Get Here?" intertwined.

Abigail's husband was Nabal, a very wealthy man. King David sent his men to Nabal to request supplies for his troops. David managed to escape several times from King Saul, who God denounced. David's servants informed Nabal of the King's protection for Nabal's shepherds and asked for resources. Nabal, a foolish drunkard, denies David's request even though David watched over his men. Nabal refused a desperate man on the run and a known warrior. Hearing his men's report, David sets out to kill every male within the household of Nabal.

Every male in Nabal's care, whether a son or an employee, was in danger of being killed until one of the servants went to Abigail. She risked everything! Abigail risked the fury of her husband and the possibility of being killed by David. She privately and quickly prepared to intercede on her household's behalf. Abigail did not say, let me pray about it first, or I will pray and let God handle this mess my husband brought on himself. I can only imagine she prayed, although the text does not state it. Prayer is always imperative.

Abigail must have proven her capabilities before this event for the servant to trust Abigail and follow her commands. Abigail physically could not manage the number of supplies. Therefore, she ordered the servants, employees to prepare for King David. She gave leadership to protect the household, but Abigail also bravely set out to address King David. Her intellect and understanding gained David's trust, which in turn saved her family and husband. Unfortunately, the hand of God turned against Nabal.

Abigail's decision to be a host of good works saved her household. She later became one of David's wives after Nabal died. No, this is not a lesson on how to get rid of your spouse to find your Boaz. It was never Abigail's intention to disrespect her husband or divorce him. She did not disregard him as she waited to tell him the events at the right time. Abigail's love for her household motivated her actions. She knew her husband as well as King David's reputation. Abigail strategically and selflessly allowed God to use her and respected her husband in the process. She did not let her emotions lead. Abigail knew how to plan and put a plan in action.

If Abigail had not interceded, an enormous amount of bloodshed would have occurred to innocent people. As children of God, it is our spiritual duty to intervene and step up so that evil does not spread, harming those who cannot help themselves. Sometimes we believe it is every man for himself or adults who need to fight their own battles. At times, it is true. However, the people Abigail saved were an entire household and staff of adults.

Like Abigail, we must know when God is putting the task in our hands to manage. We may be required to lead or follow. But the option of never doing "good works" is off the table. When God's people decide to come together, we will see spiritual strongholds broken in families, churches, and societies. If we labor only in the prayer closet, the strength of our prayers fails.

To operate in God's power, we must throw off the mentality that someone else can do it or refuse involvement because of a personal connection. Let us not wait until evil hits our families only before we decide to call out unrighteousness.

While molestation, spousal abuse, spiritual abuse, laws written to oppress the lesser population, and leaders are refusing accountability are on the rise, evil rules our societies. Whether a homemaker or CEO of a major company, each position we hold in life requires stewardship. God will call our hands for the decisions we make. For in a little while, the Master will return. He will either judge us as "good and faithful" or "wicked and slothful" (Matthew 25:14-30). We must take what God gives and use it to its full potential. Every ounce of the gifts requires careful consideration of how each skill is managed.

It is never a desire to see others without employment or resources for themselves and their families. However, our feelings towards a person should not dictate if we will follow God's lead. We must remember we are not responsible for their choices, just the ones we make.

Many times, we allow others to do wrong because they are "family" or close acquaintances. Allowing others to harm is the same as doing the injustice yourself. We are connected more spiritually than we are by blood. Jesus taught that whoever does my Father's will in heaven is my brother or sister, or mother (Matthew 12:46-50).

Those who accepted and covered Bernadine's actions are just as responsible for the harm she did and any damage she chooses to do in her new position.

Chapter 20

"Now unto Him Who's Able"

We learn early in life the difference between right and wrong. We try to follow what is right, mostly for others' approval, as we have been trained to desire. This approval allowed us to fit into societal norms. Choosing right over wrong paved our path to accolades. Flags of acceptance waved from those who love you gleefully flew and propelled you to continue moving. Encouraging cheers helped you pull through the inclines and stride in the valleys. It is like a high school student who finally realized that certain daily practices must be put in place to win friendships and popularity. Therefore, the tangible is the platform to continue.

Rightness often transforms with society and cultural expectations. Once upon a time, stores being closed on Sundays were the right thing to do. An unwed mother called to apologize in front of church members was the right thing to do. In some families and churches, hiding sexual abuse and assault was the right thing to do. We were not to expose "family business." Calling someone retarded instead of intellectually disable or challenged was once acceptable. As we evolve, what is right can and often vacillates.

Since rightness can vacillate, how can we make sure the actions taken are within God's will? The dividing line is obedience. For the Christian, we choose to believe that the Bible

"...is given by inspiration of God and is profitable for doctrine." Unfortunately, our daily practices can conflict with the remaining of the scripture, "...for reproof, for correction, for instruction in righteousness. That man (people) may be perfect thoroughly furnished unto all good works" (2 Tim. 3:16-17). Scriptural applications rest on our obedience to God. Instead of Jesus stating, "if you love me, be right," He commanded that if we loved Him, obey His commands.

The inner workings of obedience are relational between God and each person. The Biblical account of the sisters, Mary and Martha, gives a prime example of the right expectations compared to obedience. Examining Martha's inner discord with Mary, Martha is certain that her feelings are justified. Martha expected her sister to serve the guests and attempted to convince Jesus to reprimand Mary for not living up to expectations.

Martha obviously saw Mary's actions are wrong and hers as right. Perhaps Martha had reasons such as cultural norms, family expectations, or being insecure or physically tired from serving alone. What was "right" from Martha's perspective was unfruitful, according to Jesus.

Responding to Martha's attempt to involve Him in a family dispute, Jesus stated, "Martha, Martha, you are worried and troubled about many things. But one thing is needed, and Mary has chosen the good part, and it will not be taken away from her" (Luke 10:38-42).

What seemed wrong to Martha was obedience to Jesus. Jesus did not give into Martha's emotional demand. Jesus demonstrated once again that man shall not live by bread alone, but by every word that proceeds from the mouth of God. Martha received Jesus in her home but did not abide in Him though He was available to her.

Serving Jesus or her guests was not a practice of evil, but it was possibly the foundation of wrong worship, which is idolatry.

Martha's focus was making sure every guests' physical need was met. Martha may have fallen into believing that her works were the key to the relationship with Jesus if she found acceptance and service approval. Martha's service to others could have become her true worship.

More so, this thought process would have minimized Martha's life to cooking and cleaning. In correcting Martha, Jesus gave her the best of Him and a better future for her. Again, we see that love is not always an agreement to do what the other wants.

It is through Christ we learn what works are necessary for our lives. Without the Word of God, we cannot do God's work because it is the Word of God that determines and supports our work. Therefore, we scurry about doing things that matter physically but may not have any spiritual benefits for those we serve or ourselves. Busyness does not equate to fruitfulness. Busyness impedes our ability to be fruitful and multiply because we lose connection with what matters to Christ. Martha's worrying and distractions served no purpose, not even for herself.

Mary, sitting at Jesus' feet, received the Word, the bread of life. Mary's focus was on Christ and allowed Jesus to feed her spiritually. By opening her "home," her heart, to Jesus, Mary walked in obedience. She rested in Christ and was not distracted by the expectations of Martha or her guests. Mary gets Jesus' approval, acceptance, and protection to maintain her position.

Yes, we are to serve others in various ways, but service should not override the spiritual connection with Christ. Feeding on the Word of God gives direction and helps us to serve our purpose as needed daily. Obedience in relationship with Christ supersedes cultural expectations, social norms, and others' expectations. Mary chose to place Jesus first.

Our obedience is relational, but it will never contradict God's written Word. Some believe God has told them something unusual apart from His written Word. When God speaks, it will be in relation to His Word, not in contrast. Jesus spoke this truth when He taught, "Do not think that I have come to destroy the Law or the Prophets. I did not come to destroy but fulfill" (Matthew 5:17). Jesus did not change the Word of God to suit Himself. He completed what the Prophets prophesied, and our spiritual forefathers modeled as priests concerning Him and ushered in a new covenant for us.

Our new covenant, the New Testament, with God through Jesus, is our purpose. Our primary function is to "Go ye therefore, and teach all nations, baptizing them in the name of the Father, the Son, and of the Holy Ghost" (Matthew 28:19). Our daily routines such as our jobs, grocery stores, dry cleaners, churches, family get-togethers, etc. will give opportunities to fulfill Jesus' command. As these opportunities present themselves, we may be afraid, but we must learn to trust that God will provide the grace to help us through our fears. We believe His Word as He spoke them to Paul, "My grace is sufficient for you, for my power is made perfect in your weakness" (2 Corinthians 12:9).

Now that Jesus saved us, we are free to use His grace for the works of God as Jude, the half-brother of Jesus, encouraged and not profane His grace through lewdness, ungodly living (Jude 1:4). Jude wrote to fellow Christians, warning them about wicked men who have secretly come in to influence them, causing a denial of Christ.

Before Jude goes into a flashback, he urged the people to "contend for the faith." Jude explained through known examples to his audience that what we do daily enacts God's judgment. Jude did not speak to those who did not know God, but those who knew Him. The examples Jude used came from previous books, for us, the Old Testament. He knew his audience was aware of their history. This history connected and reminded them of God's character and unaccepting nature of persistent disobedience.

We believe if we confess Christ, that is all that matters. The confession is imperative. Jude gave the descriptive lifestyles of those who used God's grace as the freedom to deny Christ. If anyone knew and understood how to reject Christ, it was Jesus' brothers. Matthew 7:5 shined a light on how Jesus' brothers did not believe in Him. Mark 3:21 shared that Jesus' family considered Him out of His mind. Jude's belief changed, and he called himself a bondservant of Jesus Christ (Jude 1:1). Jude's past qualified his appeal to the children of God to live for Christ and contend earnestly for the faith, which is to struggle with sincere and intense conviction.

To contend earnestly for the faith can be the catalyst for Christians to reflect on a closer relationship with Christ or the catalyst that turns Christians away. We live in a society that relishes ease and comfort, finds security in material things, and rely on the tangible things as proof of success. The motivation to live in such a way, can compromise our faith to fit in, not rock the boat, and save ourselves from what may cause loss of earthly possessions. We are taught "favor ain't fair" without knowledge and understanding.

Favor is most often not about getting what you want. God's favor is Divine intervention and protection to do His will. Of course, He provides material things and gives us the ability to gain wealth (Deuteronomy 8:18). However, gaining material things is not God's only or principal purpose for our lives, especially if we do not use our resources to further the Kingdom's agenda.

It is not a new-age problem but has existed since the beginning of man. Adam and Eve craved more than what God gave. The desire to want more against God's purposes caused Adam and Eve shame and death, separation from God. Before the Enemy slipped in and deceived Eve, paradise was at their disposal. God's own Spirit prepared everything that was needed to be successful in the garden. It was an intricate masterpiece, as well as a relationship between and for them.

Imagine being in a mansion of your choice given to you. On the estate, there is every kind of fruit, vegetable, and herb known to man. With these vegetables, fruit, and herb seasonings, every meal was delectable. Protein was within reach and plentiful. The estate is so large that even if your spouse got on your nerves, you could hide behind large banana leaves or giant forest ferns. If that was not enough peace, you have enough land to build a getaway. You also have a personal zoological garden and calm blue water rivers running throughout. You are not afraid of the various species of land or marine animals, or birds because of your relationship with them. You named each animal by name; they respect you as a master. The grounds are fertile, and all you must do is maintain it—no mean bosses. You were born into entrepreneurship, luxury, and stability. Not only did you have all this, but you also were given the perfect companion for friendship and enjoyment.

God made and arranged a marriage for Adam and Eve, creating the first equally yoked companionship. Adam did not have to search for years, then pray all night to decide if Eve was the right one. He did not have to wonder if Eve would share his passions and dreams. Nor did Adam suffer to create a pleasant home and provisions to Eve's liking. Eve did not have to give Adam an ultimatum and pry him to put a ring on it. She did not have anyone asking how long he was going to make her wait. No games. No fights. No premarital counseling. No financial concerns. No losing weight to fit the dress. Just a handcrafted, spiritual, perfect union created by the Most Holy God in the ultimate paradise setting.

The best of all, God, the Creator the Universe, and life, gave Himself to Adam and Eve by private visitation. He walked and talked with Adam and Eve. However, Adam and Eve wanted more, so they gave up authentic security and companionship for the perception of more. Hence, we can understand why Jude pleaded with Christians to contend earnestly for the faith. Without the struggle to stay connected with God's Divine purposes, we are deceived by those who creep in with worldly ambitions and lure us into ungodly lifestyles.

We miss God's best for the misguided perception of the best. A lost spiritual connection with God brings death. Death of our Divine purpose, death of our peace, death of authentic joy, and, most importantly, the death of an intimate relationship with God. It is equivalent to Mark 8:3, "What does it profit a man if he should gain the world, and lose His soul?" The last thing any Christian should desire is anything which separates God's Spirit from us.

Disobedience can do just that. Study what happened to King Saul in 1 Samuel. Saul made choices that changed the trajectory of his Divine purpose. He failed to meet the conditions outlined by God.

Jude urged his readers not to take God's grace for granted, gave examples of the denial of Jesus, and what causes God's wrath. Afterward, he guided his audience without direction in how to contend for the faith. Jude points out three main ways to contend for the faith: by building yourself up, praying in the Holy Spirit, and keeping yourself in God's love as you wait for the mercy of Jesus Christ (Jude 1:20).

It is expected by many, to accomplish any goal, we must know how to self-encourage. It is the same for spiritual vitality. It is common to use Jesus as scriptural applications. However, many people feel inadequate or unmotivated when compared to Jesus, One who knew no sin. Some think Jesus did not live the human experience of temptations, disappointments, or rejection. We know about the cross as we hear Sunday after Sunday preachers who bring their sermons to harmonic closures or an all-inclusive summons.

The repetitional preaching of Jesus dying on the cross does not have the intended emotional effect of gratitude for many. Thank God the Blood never loses Its power regardless of whether we connect emotionally.

The common phrase, "Well, I ain't Jesus," is usually our way of saying we are not perfect, and we go forward with our desires. But Jude, a fallen man, compelled believers to contend for the faith. A gospel he did not always believe.

Jesus' life and brothers' denial of Him parallels the story of a favorite father's son, Joseph, sold into slavery by his very own brothers. Joseph later became his brothers' saving grace (Genesis 37). Though Jesus' brothers once doubted and rejected Him, His life became their saving grace and ours. Jude understood we must strive to get to know Christ.

When we get to know Him, Jesus becomes the Rock in which we build the foundation of our lives. Consistent Bible reading and Bible study, prayer, journaling, fellowship with a church body, and walking with God's will in mind will build a relationship with God through Christ Jesus. The path of righteousness is acting in God's way, regardless of the outcome. It is seeing God as Father, and not just Provider. Many parents are disappointed when their children only come to visit, expecting something needed or wanted. Frequent encounters and shared experiences build strong bonds and understanding. It is the same with God as He desires our presence secretly and corporately.

Praying in the Holy Spirit is another part of Jude's exhortation. Praying in the Holy Spirit can be speaking in other tongues, unknown languages. Whether in a foreign tongue or native to you, praying in the Holy Spirit is to pray those things aligned with God's Spirit and Word. The prerequisite of this kind of praying is Bible study.

The Bible guides us in how to pray and what to pray. Without understanding God's will, we will pray selfishly and ineffectively. For example, we often hear the scripture, "I can do all things through Christ who strengthens me," to accomplish goals or obtain material comforts (Philippians 4:13). Reading the scripture in context, the author, Paul, informs us how he learned to be content in whatever condition he finds himself, needs met or unmet. If a person used the scripture with the expectation of whatever wanted, he could obtain, then he may find despair in Christ instead of hope. It may appear that scriptures are not true out of context. However, if we read and study, then the scriptures have more clarity.

Praying in the Spirit becomes more effective because we grow in understanding of how and what to pray. Many are angry with God daily for lack of biblical teaching, consistent Bible study, and being in a church where the focus is God's Word. Without knowing God's character, we will not know what to expect from Him. If I believe Christians do not suffer, as I once did, then I would have thought Brock and Mandy's actions were a result of my wrongdoing. Instead of praying for direction and strategy, I would have wasted time praying for forgiveness.

When we understand Christ, God's Son, suffered even before the cross, we realize some of our sufferings are not a result of what we do, but Whose we are. God desires to show His power and glory through us. God promises if we remain in Him, He will make His home within us (John 15:7).

Jude includes, "...keeping yourself in the love of God, looking for the mercy of our Lord Jesus Christ unto eternal life." Love discussed earlier requires truth. To keep ourselves in the love of God, we must be reflective in correctly understanding our actions.

Love is not just a part of our emotions, as many believe between God and man. Love is the balance of correction, giving, receiving, sacrifice, and, most importantly, repenting. Love is gratitude, acceptance, and worship to our Creator, which can be emotional as we reflect on His goodness and mercy despite our sins. To keep ourselves in God's love, we submit ourselves to His will.

Many days, I agonized from the emotional weight of the situation with Lowland ISD. Without any doubt, I knew the trial was God's doing and not of my own. Since I understood this, then it was a matter of am I a friend of God or a friend of the world? The determining factor was where I placed my allegiance. If I chose my career, others' opinions, or home (material things) over God's call for this moment, then I became an enemy towards God (James 4:4). To love what the world offers more than God's will is putting those things before God. Our love for God obligates us to do His work. That was my motivation throughout the tears, doubts, feeling crazy, and feeling alone, which kept me from giving up.

Looking to complete my race through the mercy of Jesus in which eternal life also helped me to focus on obedience. It is not by works we are saved, but by works, our faith is expressed. "Faith without works is dead (James 2:14-26). Faith connects our race to other believers like a relay. Each person ordained by God has a specific leg in the race.

When I reported the child's incident to the district's superintendent and CPS twice, I passed the baton. When I wrote the letter of racial discrimination and workplace harassment, I passed the baton again. When I asked to view the videos and requested them from the Attorney General, I passed the baton. When I wrote to the Texas Education Agency regarding educator misconduct, I passed the baton. When I walked alone into the district's attorney's office to discuss my claim, I passed the baton.

Like Moses to Pharaoh before the exodus from Egypt or Deborah to Barak, the receiver had the choice for how they would "contend for the faith." Whether or not each receiver claims God as Lord does not matter, for each of us will be held accountable for the responsibility of dropping or carrying the baton.

We must also realize when our part is completed. Once completed and the baton is handed off, it is not our responsibility or ability to force people to run their legs. It is very unsettling when it appears as though the work was in vain because we do not physically see the result.

Since we often operate and are motivated by results, we feel compelled to quit. Like when losing weight, the results motivate us to continue. We attend college or trade schools for the result of earning more money. We follow recipes for the results to come out pleasing and tasteful. It is in our control. However, spiritual matters are not result-oriented that are always seen physically. We walk by faith and not by sight (2 Corinthians 5:7). Again, we must rely on our relationship with God through obedience to know it is well.

I hesitated in writing this book until I saw results. Sure, I saw Brock and Mandy transferred to different locations. Lowland ISD stated my evidence of racism, discrimination, and hostile workplace was sufficient, at least against Brock. I saw how the Texas Education Agency required additional ethics training for every school district employee. I witnessed the district withholding both requested videos. No one hides without cause. I learned one of the leaders named in the letter left the district. However, it was not the results I expected or sometimes desired.

When in moments of despair about the situation, I encouraged myself by remembering a song taught to our church by the minister of music, "Daily, I Shall Worship Thee." My worship is daily. My worship is my obedience to contend for the faith. My worship is to release every skill, gift, and energy to benefit the Kingdom of God. My brothers and sisters, let us trust God will do as Jude concluded his letter, "To Him Who is able to keep you from stumbling and present you before His glorious presence without fault and with great joy. To the only God, our Savior be glory, majesty, power, and authority, through Jesus Christ, our Lord, before all ages, now and forevermore! Amen" (Jude 1: 24-25). Daily, contend for the faith.

Acknowledgments

Many people encouraged me throughout my Journey for Justice. To my middle school department colleagues, thank you for the constant listening ear, understanding, and a plethora of encouraging words and prayers. Thank you for all the many counseling sessions in the "corner room." To my elementary colleagues, thank you for your kindness, allowing me to learn as a school counselor, and receive counsel from many of you.

To my cousin, Dr. Rosetta Jones, thank you for stating on Facebook you could not wait until my first book. You had no idea this book was in the works!

To my sisters and best friends, Wanda, Sandra, and April, you all are the absolute best! God showed out when He gave me you all. To my brother, John Jr., your words, "I hope in the time of adversity, I will stand like my little sister," meant the world to me. It gave me confidence that God was pleased. To my parents, especially my mother, you are the epitome of beauty, perseverance, and hope. Thank you both for allowing me to learn and grow into the purpose of the One who knitted me together. You did more talking and teaching as a disciplinary method.

To my church family, the loving Mt. Zion Baptist Church in Forney, Texas, you all are the best! Your genuine care for my family created an unbreakable bond. Thank each of you for walking the path with us. Most importantly, thank you for allowing me to be comfortable and accepted "just as I am."

To all the gospel ministers, whether in preaching, teaching, or music, may God bless you exceedingly and abundantly! What you do matters! Your work soothes anxiety, confirms God's love and protection. It is the beacon of light the world needs.

To Esther Walker Bullard, thank you for never failing to assist. You immediately connected me to the best lawyer in the industry. I continue in prayer for you.

To Diane Jimerson, thank you for reconnection and encouragement during a critical moment.

To all my early readers, thank you for your time and input. You helped guide the writing. Your support and encouragement blessed me.

To Perry Fair, thank you for "that."

Last but definitely not least, to husband and Pastor, Robert McElroy, thank you for your companionship, friendship, and leadership. Your dedication to the truth of God's word, teaching, and leading with love is unmatched. Thank you for covering and making sure the family's needs are met in every area to the best of your abilities. May God increase your territory!

To the fantastic four, Dawn, Tye, Aaren, and Michael, thank you for being the better part of me. May God show you what I see within each of you. As Dr. Charles Stanley teaches, "Obey God and leave the consequences to Him." Life is a journey, but He promises to never leave or forsake you. Believe Him! Heaven is our goal.

To the unknown who tried to make the right decision when I sent the letter, thank you. I still believe there had to have been at least one.

To my heavenly Father, may You be pleased. Let all I say and do honor You in Jesus' name. Thank you for loving me, unconditionally. I give you all of me.

A Note on the Text

This book is a work of memoir. Although more events occurred than could be recounted, the author chose significant events for the narrative. The letter written in chapter 11 is mostly unedited for the purpose of helping the reader to understand that it is more important to act than to shy away in imperfection.

Names of people, schools, and the school district were changed because it is the overall message that the author wishes to convey, not exposure. Though public records are usually accessible legally, the author realizes that media extends beyond our times. The families of the individuals did not make the leaderships' choices and do not deserve the connection.

As of September 24, 2020, a follow-up report from CPS has not occurred.

Appendix

List of Agencies Sought for Assistance

Texas Education Agency (TEA)

Texas State Board of Education (SBEC)

Texas Workforce Commission

U.S. Dept. of Education Civil Rights

U. S. Equal Employment Opportunity Commission (EEOC)

Texas Attorney General Open Records

Child Protective Services/Dallas Division

About the Author

Darline Amos-McElroy was born and raised in Leland, MS. She received her B.S. in Biology from the University of Arkansas at Pine Bluff, Arkansas. Shortly after graduating, she transplanted to Dallas, Texas, where she became a wife, mother, an educator, school counselor, and a Licensed Professional Counselor. Darline resides with her husband, Pastor Robert B. McElroy, and children in the suburbs of Dallas, Texas. I Ate the Cake: A Journey for Justice is Darline's debut writing.

Made in the USA
Coppell, TX
04 March 2021